HARDCORE CATFISHING

Beyond the Basics

Keith "Catfish" Sutton

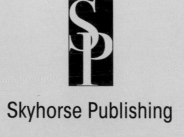

Skyhorse Publishing

Skyhorse Publishing books may be purchased in bulk at special discounts for sales promotion, corporate gifts, fund-raising, or educational purposes. Special editions can also be created to specifications. For details, contact the Special Sales Department, Skyhorse Publishing, 307 West 36th Street, 11th Floor, New York, NY 10018 or info@skyhorsepublishing.com.

Skyhorse® and Skyhorse Publishing® are registered trademarks of Skyhorse Publishing, Inc.®, a Delaware corporation.

Visit our website at www.skyhorsepublishing.com.

10 9 8 7 6 5 4 3 2

Library of Congress Cataloging-in-Publication Data is available on file.

Cover design by Richard Rossiter
Cover photo credit Keith Sutton

Art: Duane Raver, U.S. Fish and Wildlife Service

Print ISBN: 978-1-62914-601-0
Ebook ISBN: 978-1-62914-899-1

Printed in China

To Alex Hinson, bourbon, and campfires, my companions through many a long night of catfishing.

Contents

Introduction

"… the catfish is a plenty good enough fish for anybody …"

Mark Twain wrote that in 1883 when catfish were at the peak of their popularity. In fact, prior to the 1960s largemouth-bass fishing boom, Americans always looked upon catfish as highly desirable sport and food fish.

That changed when bass tournaments became the rage, and anglers began focusing more attention on trout, walleyes, and other fish. Catfish anglers became nonentities. Most tackle manufacturers ignored them. The outdoor media snubbed them. Some even tried to shame them.

All the while, however, Americans continued catfishing. Throughout the 1960s, 1970s, and 1980s, catfish maintained their position as the country's third most popular fish. Only black bass and panfish were more in demand. Such is still the case today.

In recent years, anglers, manufacturers, and media realized they no longer could ignore these whiskered pole-benders' many positive attributes. Catfish are widespread, abundant, grow large (130 pounds and heavier), eagerly take a variety of baits, fight hard, and are delicious. What's not to like?

Number and Distribution of Catfish Anglers

According to the US Fish and Wildlife Service's *2006 National Survey of Fishing, Hunting, and Wildlife-Associated Recreation*, approximately 6.95 million US anglers age sixteen and older fish for catfish, 27.3 percent of our 25.4 million adult freshwater anglers.

More than half of all US catfish anglers (3.99 million) reside in just ten states: Texas (1.035 million), Missouri (448,000), Georgia (395,000), Florida (389,000), Illinois (335,000), Tennessee (298,000), North Carolina (294,000), Ohio (288,000), Oklahoma (264,000), and Alabama (245,000). But catfish also are popular in states with fewer anglers. In Nebraska, for example, no other fish are more sought with 69,000 catfish anglers statewide. Catfish rank second in popularity behind black bass or panfish in Arkansas (235,000 anglers), Mississippi (218,000), Kansas (216,000), Iowa (214,000), and Louisiana (207,000).

Most catfish anglers reside in the South or Midwest where catfish are most plentiful. The fewest live in the Northeast and West, which are regions at the periphery of catfish range with fewer fish available. Ten states report few to no catfish anglers: Alaska, Connecticut, Hawaii, Maine, Montana, New Hampshire, North Dakota, Rhode Island, Vermont, and Wyoming. Catfish also rank low in popularity in Colorado, Delaware, Idaho, Maryland, Massachusetts, Michigan, Minnesota, New Jersey, New York, Nevada, Oregon, Pennsylvania, South Dakota, Utah, Washington, and Wisconsin.

Demographics

Few angler surveys have been conducted to ascertain the demographics of catfish anglers. One was conducted in 2010 in Texas, a state where catfish exceed even black bass in popularity. No other state has as many catfish anglers (1,035,000) or a larger percentage of anglers who target catfish (56 percent).

About 51 percent of survey respondents preferred fishing for channel catfish, 35 percent preferred blues, and 12 percent preferred flatheads. Only 2 percent had no preference or preferred bullheads.

On average, respondents had been catfish anglers twenty-nine years and spent twenty days annually catfishing. Approximately 65 percent of trips were spent fishing from a boat and 35 percent from shore. One-third of trips included night fishing. Eighty-one percent used a rod and reel most often, 9 percent used trotlines, 7 percent jug lines, and 3 percent limb lines.

A 2001 Missouri survey provided demographics for the nation's number-two catfishing state (448,000 catfish anglers). Show-Me State catfish anglers are primarily male (79 percent), between ages thirty-six and fifty-five (52 percent), and live mostly (73 percent) in rural communities or small towns (73 percent). Seventy-five percent favored channel catfish, 14 percent flatheads, 9 percent blue catfish, and 2 percent bullheads. More than 80 percent preferred fishing with rod and reel. When asked to choose which scenario (i.e., one twenty-pound catfish, two 10-pound catfish, four 5-pound catfish, or ten 2-pound catfish) best described the number and size of catfish they preferred to catch and keep, most preferred four 5-pound catfish or ten 2-pound catfish. However, age influenced responses. Catfish anglers younger than thirty-five years old preferred catching fewer but larger catfish. Anglers older than fifty-five preferred catching more but smaller catfish.

A 2001 survey of catfish anglers throughout the Mississippi River basin found fishing for fun was the most important reason respondents fished, but catching bigger fish enhanced their trip. More than 70 percent took at least one trip annually to pursue trophy catfish. Trophy anglers preferred blue and flathead catfish, whereas non-trophy anglers preferred channel catfish.

Despite many similarities between catfish anglers and other anglers, a 1999 Mississippi survey found fundamental differences. Catfish anglers, as compared with those fishing for largemouth bass, crappie, and sunfish, placed more importance on harvest levels and catching large fish while showing the least support for harvest restrictions. This survey also discovered catfish anglers had more diversity in age, gender, and ethnic backgrounds than other anglers.

Catfishing Today

Catfishing is extremely varied. Participants fish night and day, year-round, for big fish and small, from boats and shore, using natural and artificial baits on everything from ultralight combos to heavy-action bait-casting rigs, plus trotlines, jugs, and limblines. Nevertheless, today's catfish anglers fall within two basic categories: those targeting smaller catfish (usually channel cats) to eat or those targeting big catfish (blues and flatheads) primarily for sport.

"Folks who want to catch a few cats and take them home to a hot skillet are still the mainstay in catfishing," said Jeff Williams, owner of Team Catfish Tackle in Grove, Oklahoma. "They greatly outnumber trophy anglers, but availability of high-quality educational information through the Internet and other media has created a new breed of trophy-catfish angler. Info on catching big cats was guarded by old timers in the past but now streams across televisions and computer monitors like water through a faucet. The desire to tangle with a true giant, a catfish over fifty pounds, is what this new breed is laser-focused on."

T.J. Stallings, director of marketing for TTI Blakemore Fishing Group in Wetumpka, Alabama, concurs. "Unlike bass fishing, catfishing doesn't need that 'perfect cast,' so novices can jump into the sport with relative ease," he said. "The biggest attraction, however, is the battle. Nothing in freshwater fights like a large blue or flathead. Once an angler lands a big cat, he can't wait to do it again."

So how do you fit into this picture? I pose the question, but the answer really doesn't matter. No matter what type of catfish you hope to catch—channel cats, blues, flatheads, or bullheads, big cats or small, cats to keep and eat, or trophy catfish you battle and release. In the pages that follow, you'll learn top-notch cat-catching techniques developed by America's most innovative catfish guides and anglers. You'll read scientific information about catfish behavior and how it affects your fishing. You'll discover baits, rigs, and tactics used by the catfishermen of yesteryear that are still highly effective today. You'll master regional catfishing tactics that, until now, haven't been widely known. And through it all, if I've done my job well, you'll enjoy a chuckle now and then, an occasional surprise, and a good read all the way through.

I hope *Hardcore Catfishing* lives up to your expectations. It's been fun to write. Good fishing.

Keith "Catfish" Sutton

About the Author

Keith Sutton didn't earn the nickname "Catfish" for nothing. This is his fifth book about catfishing. His passion for the sport has taken him to blue-ribbon catfishing waters throughout the United States and in Mexico, Canada, Venezuela, and Brazil. His special insights about catching these whiskered warriors were garnered through fifty years of on-the-water research and countless hours of discussions with biologists, researchers, and expert anglers.

Sutton is a prolific freelance writer, photographer, editor, and lecturer with more than 3,500 feature articles published in *Outdoor Life, Field & Stream, Sports Afield, Cabela's Outfitter Journal, North American Fisherman, In-Fisherman,* and many other state, regional, and national periodicals. His works as an award-winning photographer have been featured in a broad spectrum of books, magazines, newspapers, and calendars. In 2011, he was inducted into the National Freshwater Fishing Hall of Fame as a Legendary Communicator.

Sutton lives in Alexander, Arkansas, with his wife Theresa. They have six sons. Visit his Web site at www.catfishsutton.com.

Zeroing in on Channel Cats

Facts About Channel Catfish

The channel cat is the pin up of the catfish world—sleek, muscular, and one of the best reasons to be a kid with school out and a good fishing hole nearby.

If you like catfishing, chances are good you love the channel catfish (*Ictalurus punctatus*). This freckle-flanked, mid-sized cat is targeted by more anglers than any other species thanks largely to its abundance and extensive range. Most anglers who pursue the species do so because channel cats are incredibly delicious, and they want some fish to take home and eat. But everyone who targets this whiskered warrior also enjoys

its truculent nature, savoring to the utmost the water-churning skirmishes that always ensue when a channel cat is on the line.

Description

Channel cats aren't colorful fish. The back and sides are silvery-gray to coppery-brown, speckled with a few too many small black spots. The belly is white. The tail has a deep fork. Breeding

Channel catfish as big as this pair from Manitoba's Red River are uncommon except in a few extraordinary waters.

Channel catfish

Food Habits

Until they reach about twelve inches long, channel cats feed extensively on large aquatic insects, small fish, and a variety of invertebrates, such as terrestrial insects, crayfish, and mussels. Fish such as minnows, chubs, and other catfish comprise a larger part of the diet when channel cats exceed a foot in length, but as they grow, the catfish continue chowing down on invertebrates and other available foods. The bigger a channel cat becomes, however, the more fish it is apt to eat. By the time it reaches several pounds in weight, a channel cat subsists almost entirely on other fish.

males take on a deep blue-black hue, and their head becomes greatly enlarged with thickened jowls and lips.

Blue cats are very similar in appearance but rarely exhibit the black speckling seen on all but the oldest channel cats. The best way to distinguish the two species is to examine the anal fin. On channel cats, this fin has twenty-four to twenty-nine rays and a rounded outer edge. Blue cats have a straight-edged anal fin with thirty or more rays.

Size

In July 1964, an angler fishing in South Carolina's Lake Moultrie caught a forty-seven-inch-long channel cat that weighed fifty-eight pounds. That world record still stands, and many experts believe it will never be broken. Only four states—South Carolina, Arkansas, Mississippi, and California—have produced channel cats exceeding fifty pounds, and in no place are channel cats that size regularly caught.

In waters with healthy channel cat populations, one- to five-pounders tend to be abundant and six- to ten-pounders only slightly less common. To catch a channel cat that exceeds fifteen pounds, however, is quite extraordinary except in a few very productive waters. In the Red River below Lockport Dam near Selkirk, Manitoba, for example, twenty- to twenty-five-pound channel cats comprise a large percentage of the catch. Elsewhere, you can consider yourself quite lucky if you land a twenty-pounder. Thirty-pounders are as rare as twelve-pound largemouths.

Small black spots on the sides identify the channel catfish regardless of where it is caught. Some older specimen may lack these spots, however.

Range

The original range of channel catfish stretched between the Rocky and Appalachian mountains, from the Hudson Bay drainage to the Gulf of Mexico, and north and east of the Appalachian Mountains. Transplants to new waters have expanded the species' range to include every state but Alaska, plus six of the ten Canadian provinces and many lakes and rivers in Mexico as well. Channel cats are considered important sport species in at least thirty-two US states.

Habitat

Channel cats are amazingly adaptable, inhabiting nearly any body of water that's not too cold, too polluted, or too salty. Anglers catch them in everything from clear creeks, fertile farm ponds, and turbid sloughs to huge man-made reservoirs, natural lakes, and slow-moving bottomland rivers. Channel catfish thrive best in clean, warm, well-oxygenated water with slow to moderate current and abundant cover, such as logs, boulders, cavities, and debris.

Basic Fishing Tactics

A small spinning or spincast outfit spooled with six- to fifteen-pound-test monofilament line is ideal for catching channel cats you'd like to keep and eat. Upgrade to heavier tackle only if you're targeting trophy fish specifically. The other tackle you'll need can be carried in a small tackle box: a few hooks, sinkers, and bobbers, some extra line, a stringer, and some pliers for removing hooks from the catfish's tough mouth.

Any catfishing rig can be used, but the simplest usually work best. One such rig, the slip-sinker, is easily made by placing a small egg sinker on your main line above a barrel swivel tied at the line's end. Add an eighteen-inch leader to the swivel's other eye, and tie a hook (1/0 to 3/0

bait-holder, octopus or Kahle) to the end of that.

Another easy rig that works well is just a bobber above a medium-sized hook with a split shot pinched on the line between the two to sink the bait.

The list of good baits you can use is extensive. Some of the best include fresh chicken liver, night crawlers, minnows, crayfish, stinkbaits (commercial

Channel cats have a rounded anal fin with twenty-four to twenty-nine rays.

Despite popular misconceptions, channel cats feed actively year-round, even in the coldest part of winter.

and homemade), catalpa worms, shrimp, hot dogs, and frogs.

Despite what many anglers think, fishing for channel cats is not just a summer sport. You can fish year-round and expect to do well even during the coldest part of winter. Night fishing often produces more cats because they tend to be in the shallows more at night, and shallow shoreline waters are where most anglers fish. Channel cats feed actively during all hours, however, and are easily caught even during daylight hours if you fish prime hotspots, such as outside river bends, dam tailwaters, river wing dikes, and holes, tributary mouths, bottom channels, riprap, log piles, stump fields, and deep holes in ponds.

Although rod-and-reel fishing is most popular, all species of catfish are also targeted by anglers using other types of tackle, including trotlines, jugs, limb-lines, and yo-yos.

Crashin' & Thrashin'

Getting cats out of trees can be a tough job unless you know the proper technique.

The best way to learn new catfishing tricks is to pick the brains of your catfishing friends. Every hardcore cat man has special tricks and tactics no one else seems to know. One catter whose brain I've picked is Denny Halgren, a Dixon, Illinois, angler who uses unconventional tactics to get cats out of trees—channel cats, that is.

If you came upon Halgren on Illinois' Rock River, where he's guided catfishermen for more than forty years, you might wonder if he were in trouble. Chances are his boat would be smack-dab on top of a big tree laid over in the water. He might be in the boat, but more likely, he'd be standing on the tree with a rod and reel.

Some who have come upon Halgren in this situation believed he'd crashed his craft into the timber. In a way, they were right.

You see, Halgren has perfected an advanced catfishing tactic he calls crashin' and thrashin'. In a nutshell, it works like this. First, you "crash" your boat into big timber to reach those hard-to-get-at catfish hotspots other anglers wouldn't dare fish from. Next, you drop a bait into the swirling water at just the right spot. Then, if a catfish is there, you experience the thrashin' part of the name. The fish nabs the bait, you set the hook, and you try to hoss a thrashin' log kitty from its hidey-hole. Sometimes you win. Sometimes you lose. But

Dixon, Illinois, catfishing guide Denny Halgren shows a nice channel cat taken using his unique crashin' and thrashin' technique.

when you learn Halgren's technique, you'll be battling far more jumbo catfish than your still-fishing buddies.

A Tree and a Boil

The key, Halgren says, is pinpointing the exact spot where a big cat will be. Each spot has two primary components: a big tree and a big boil.

"The ideal place," he says, "is where current has undercut a tree and toppled it into the water. At least part of the tree must be in shallow water—two to three feet deep—and there must be at least moderate current coming across the tree. With the right amount of current, the biggest most territorial catfish centralize. In other words, the current causes them to hold in specific spots where they can easily grab food carried within. Without proper current, the fish could be anywhere and are difficult to

pinpoint. When the current is right, you can find them every time."

When scouting a river, look for a single fallen tree perpendicular to the bank with the root end close to shore in shallow water. A big drift pile with numerous trees would seem better. But Halgren says a thick tree that "looks like a fence post"—with few branches—may draw bigger fish.

"In the best spots, current washes beneath the tree's trunk in shallow water and creates a channel," he says. "As water goes through that channel, it's funneled through to the downstream side of the tree and creates a big boil. Right in that boil is where you want to fish. You may catch smaller catfish in other spots around the tree's perimeter. But the biggest cat on that piece of cover will almost always be in the biggest boil."

Catfishermen scouting a river for crashin' and thrashin' hot spots should watch for a single fallen tree perpendicular to the bank with the root end close to shore in shallow water.

Crashin'

The crashin' part of this technique isn't as dangerous as it sounds. Ideally, after spotting a good tree/boil location, the boat operator slows the boat and slides it gently onto the tree trunk or into the tree's branches. Done properly, the boat will catch and hold. The fisherman then can drop his bait into the boil.

"You must be positioned so you can drop your bait straight down into the largest boil on the downstream side of the trunk," says Halgren. "What's surprising to most anglers is that riding your boat up on that tree rarely spooks the fish. Big cats just don't spook, so you can move right in on top of them."

The Right Bait and Rig

When fishing woody cover, Halgren says, it's important to use bait that triggers quick hits from feeding fish. His favorite is a commercial cheese-flavored dip bait, JoJo's Pole Snatcher made by Cat Tracker Bait Company.

"There's no flour in this bait," he says, "so the bait doesn't slough off. If that happens, the catfish will eat the bait, but he won't get your hook. You can't catch him that way. The Cat Tracker bait stays on the worm where it's needed."

The "worm" Halgren refers to is a Cat Tracker Tubie 2000 or Cat Tracker Egg Worm. These special-made, soft-plastic baits are ribbed so the dip bait clings when the worm is pushed into it. The Egg Worm comes prerigged with a two-foot section of twenty-pound-test mono run through the worm and tied to a small treble hook that fits snuggly against the tail end. The Tubie 2000 is made to be rigged by the angler.

Halgren uses single 2/0 or 3/0 Tru-Turn hooks on both rigs—catfish hooks with the Tubie 2000 and worm hooks with the Egg Worm. The rig is tied to his main line—twenty-pound Stren mono—with a 1/4-ounce split shot or bullet sinker on the line above the worm. When a bullet sinker is used, a split shot is placed below it to peg it on the line.

"If I'm dropping baits into a spot with a lot of branches, I slide the weight down so it almost touches the top of the worm," Halgren says. "If the boil is behind the trunk and pretty free of

Variations of Denny Halgren's crashin' and thrashin' rig.

obstruction, I slide the weight up above the worm about six inches." This type of rig is simple and ideal for fishing in these situations. In four to five miles per hour current, the bait will stay on about forty-five minutes.

"I drop the rig in the boil then leave it," he says. "You can't move the bait, even if you think it's hung. You'll probably get a hit right away. If not, wait up to ten minutes. If you don't have a catfish by then, move and try another spot."

Thrashin'

This tactic often produces channel cats from four to twelve pounds, Halgren says. "Even though they're hefty cats, you can set the hook, keep a tight line, and get them out. Get them up, and let them thrash at the top of the water. That way they won't get wrapped up, and you can get them out."

Getting a cat out of a tree is never easy, whether it has fur or fins. You may get scratched. You could fall. You have to be brave—some say crazy—to try.

But if, like Denny Halgren, you're brave enough or crazy enough to fish where other anglers won't, big channel cats will be your prize. Crashin' and thrashin' is proven to catch cats when other tactics fail.

Fiddlers for the Table

Targeting eating-sized catfish differs considerably from trophy fishing.

When I advise people wanting to catch trophy-class catfish, I start by telling them they must be patient and persistent. Catching trophy cats doesn't happen every day, even for those thoroughly familiar with their habits. You may spend hundreds of fishless hours trying to pinpoint a single trophy fish. Sometimes you must travel long distances to reach the best waters, which are usually big rivers and reservoirs. You need high-quality tackle (often expensive), and your chances are much better if you have a boat equipped with sonar. The baits you use must be fresh and sometimes are hard to get.

When you finally do hook a trophy-class cat, that's no guarantee you'll land it. You'll probably lose as many as you catch, and the disappointments may seem overwhelming. If you do land one, it's best that you release it. After all, today's releases are tomorrow's trophies.

Some enthusiasts listen intently then pack up their tackle and head straight for a big river or lake. They love a fishing challenge, and giant cats certainly provide that.

Many folks have a different reaction, however. "I'm not interested in catching a huge fish," is

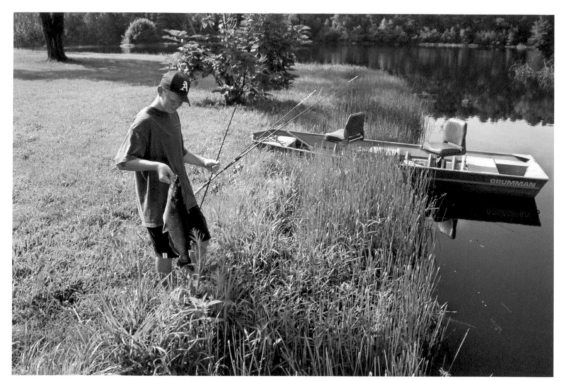

Catfish anglers usually have one goal in mind when they go fishing: catching a fish for dinner.

their typical response. "I just want to have fun and maybe catch a few fish to eat."

When you zero in on eating-sized cats, those ten pounds or fewer, the experience is vastly different than trophy fishing. Patience and persistence are rarely required because eating-sized cats are abundant in many waters, including ponds, small streams, and urban lakes. The baits you need can be bought in a grocery or discount store, and expensive gear is hardly a prerequisite. A cane pole or discount fishing combo works great.

When the cats are active (they usually are), you might catch a score or more during a few hours of leisurely bank fishing. And because smaller cats are common, you need not feel guilty keeping some to eat. In fact, keeping is encouraged. Populations do best when folks keep the little ones thinned out.

Targeting smaller catfish is also great when you're fishing with kids. Eating-sized cats are not especially wary, so your child will probably catch some even if he's got ants in his pants. A five-pound cat is on the small side in reality, but to a youngster, one that size is gigantic. Even little cats fight like blue blazes, so it's always fun. Take a kid catfishing, and you'll make memories together that will last forever.

Where to Go

Begin with a call to the freshwater fisheries department of your state wildlife agency. Ask for the names of some waters in your area that receive regular stockings of eating-sized cats. State and federal agencies stock millions of one- to two-pound catfish every year, and most will gladly send you a stocking list that shows where the fish were released. Most also

Any catfishing rig can be used, but the simplest usually work best. A slip-sinker rig, my favorite, is easily made by placing a small egg sinker on your main line above a barrel swivel tied at the line's end. Add an eighteen-inch leader to the swivel's other eye, and tie a hook (1/0 to 3/0 baitholder, octopus or Kahle) to the end of that.

Another easy rig that works well is just a bobber above a small hook with a split shot pinched on the line between the two to sink the bait.

If you need to, you can get along quite well with just a box of hooks and some bait. In catfishing circles, this is called fishing naked. The hook is tied on, baited, and cast out. The bait then sinks enticingly in the water, attracting hungry cats without any extra terminal tackle that might spook the occasional wary fish.

Bait Choices

Unlike heavyweight cats, which rarely eat anything but fish, eating-sized whiskers aren't the least bit finicky when it comes to food. Buy some worms or minnows at the bait shop or pick up some fresh chicken liver, hot dogs,

Catching a stringer full of hard-fighting, good-eating catfish will put a smile on any kid's face.

list good catfishing waters on their Web sites. Either way, you'll probably turn up several potential honey holes, including perhaps some small lakes with good bank fishing areas, fishing piers, or a little stream where you can sit in a lawn chair on shore and wait for a bite.

Tackle Tips

A small spinning or spincast outfit is ideal for this type of fishing. I keep mine spooled with six- to ten-pound-test monofilament.

The other tackle you'll need can be carried in a small tackle box: a few hooks, sinkers, and bobbers, some extra line, a stringer, and some pliers for removing hooks from the catfish's tough mouth.

Small catfish aren't finicky eaters, so bait choices are legion. Night crawlers and other good baits can be purchased at most bait shops.

bacon, cheese, or shrimp at the supermarket. Small pieces of the latter five work extremely well on bullheads, channel cats, and small blues and flatheads.

Commercial dip baits and doughbaits also work great and usually can be found in the sporting goods department of discount stores. When using these, you might want to pick up a few of the specialty items often used to fish these soft baits, including some catfish "worms" (ribbed, soft-plastic lures used for fishing dip bait, or some spring-wound doughbait treble hooks.

Exposed Hooks Work Better

You probably won't have trouble finding eating-sized cats, but beginners often are frustrated when they can't hook those that bite. It's a common complaint, but fortunately, there's a simple though often overlooked solution.

The secret is fishing with an exposed hook. Many catters think hiding the point of the hook means more cats when actually the opposite is true. Catfish don't know or care what a hook is. If you continually bury your hook in your bait, you'll miss fish more than half the time.

If you're fishing minnows, don't push the hook's barb back into the fish. Slip it once through the lips, back, or the narrow part of the tail, and leave the point exposed. If you're using worms or night crawlers, thread the hook through two or three times, but don't hide the point. Do likewise when fishing with bacon, hot dogs, or other grocery baits.

When fishing with chicken liver, here's another rigging tip. Liver has a tendency to fly off the hook, but you can overcome this problem by wrapping the liver in a small square of nylon stocking, pulling the four corners together, then threading your hook through the corners, leaving the point exposed. A treble hook attached to your line with a swivel also works. Unsnap the swivel, remove the hook, push the eye of the hook through the liver so the liver is impaled on the three barbs, then reattach the hook to the swivel.

Night or Day?

The biggest catfish often prowl more at night, but eating-sized cats are active day or night, so go fishing whenever you can. My favorite fishing period is around daybreak, five a.m. to eight a.m. There's nothing magical about this time, but on many waters, peak feeding activity occurs just as the sun is rising. Fish then, and you're almost guaranteed to increase your catch.

Seasons

Despite what many anglers think, catfishing is not just a summertime sport. In fact, you can fish year-round and expect to do well.

My favorite months for catching eating-sized cats are January and February. Many ponds in my area are stocked with channel cats and bullheads, and when the water, temperature is between forty and fifty-five degrees, these fish move to the deepest water, where they gather in huge schools. I drop a rig baited with chicken liver into the hole, let it reach the bottom, then crank the reel handle a few times so the bait is a foot or so above the substrate. The cats usually strike quickly, and in a couple hours, it's not unusual to catch fifteen to twenty weighing one to seven pounds. It's a great way to liven up a dreary winter day, and catfish never taste better than when fresh-caught from icy cold water.

Have Fun

Targeting trophy catfish is an exciting challenge no doubt. But if you're like me, there are times when you're happy just sitting under a shade tree on a lake and catching a few small cats for

Young, old, boys, girls—channel catfish are an exciting catch for anglers of all ages and sexes.

dinner. For many of us, catfishing is a way to relax or enjoy a few hours fishing with the kids. If a big cat is caught now and then, so much the better. But catching big fish is secondary to just being there, enjoying the outdoors, and tussling with a decent fish now and then.

Zero in on some eating-sized cats this season. Take your children or some kids from the neighborhood along. It's fun. It's relaxing. It's enjoyable. And as soon as you smell the aroma of those catfish fillets frying up golden and delicious, you'll be ready to do it again.

How to get the Blues

Facts About Blue Catfish

Once ignored by all but a small cadre of hardcore cat men, in recent decades the blue cat has become the target of choice for many anglers hoping to land the biggest fish of a lifetime.

Size is the attribute most responsible for the increasing popularity of the blue catfish (*Ictalurus furcatus*). The only North American freshwater fishes that grow larger are the alligator gar, lake sturgeon, and white sturgeon. However, these species have much more restricted ranges than blue cats and rarely are abundant. Anglers hoping to catch a freshwater fish weighing fifty to one-hundred pounds or more are fishing for America's widespread, abundant blue cats in greater numbers than ever before. As a result, dozens of new state and world records have been established in recent decades.

Description
The blue catfish closely resembles its channel cat cousin. The slate-blue to grayish-brown back and sides fade to a whitish belly. The tail is deeply forked. On blue cats, however, the anal fin contains more rays—usually thirty

In recent years, more and more anglers have begun pursuing the blue catfish, one of North America's most abundant, widespread heavyweight sportfish.

Blue catfish

to thirty-five as compared to the channel cat's twenty-four to twenty-nine—and has a straight, not rounded, outer margin. In muddy environments, some blue cats appear albino, the pale skin evoking the common nickname

A straight-edge anal fin, shaped much like an old-fashioned barber's comb, helps identify this as a blue catfish.

This blue cat weighed 72 pounds. The species has the potential to grow more than twice this size.

"white cat." Other colloquial names include blue fulton, white fulton, blue channel, and humpback cat. Many individuals also are distinctly humpbacked in appearance and have a head much smaller in proportion to the body than a similarly-sized channel cat.

Size

Healthy populations of blue cats usually contain numerous individuals up to twenty-eight inches or about ten pounds. Larger older fish are less common, but in some prime waters, catching several twenty- to forty-pound blues during a few hours of fishing is not considered unusual during peak fishing times. The largest specimens, those weighing fifty pounds or

more, are much scarcer and often difficult to find and catch, but more and more anglers enjoy the challenge of targeting these big hard-hitting trophies. Nothing can prepare an angler for their astonishing power. These Goliaths fry drags, bust rods, and snap line like sewing thread. A really big one can pummel an angler till his arms and legs tremble.

In recent decades, blues exceeding one hundred pounds have been caught from waters in several states, including Alabama, Arkansas, California, Illinois, Indiana, Kansas, Kentucky, Louisiana, Missouri, Oklahoma, South Carolina, Tennessee, Texas, and Virginia. Fishing in Virginia's Kerr Reservoir on June 18, 2011, Nick Anderson of Greenville, North Carolina, landed the current all-tackle world record, a massive 55-inch-long blue that weighed 143 pounds.

Food Habits

Blue catfish are opportunistic feeders, consuming a variety of animals that include fishes, insects, crayfish, and freshwater mussels. Larger individuals eat mostly fish and larger invertebrates. They are particularly fond of shad, herring, and other schooling baitfish and often are found associated with schools of these baitfish. Blue cats frequently suspend in deep water beneath shad being eaten by striped bass, picking off the wounded and dead baitfish left by the stripers. They also feed on wounded baitfish that pass through the turbines of dams and baitfish killed by cold winter temperatures.

Blues seem intermediate between the other two species of big cats in feeding habits, not insisting on live baits as flatheads do but generally ignoring many specialty offerings, such as stinkbaits and blood baits, often used to catch channel cats. Blue cats feed year-round except during spawning activities. Feeding diminishes, however, when the water temperature falls below forty degrees Fahrenheit.

Range

Blue cats occur in twenty-nine states from South Dakota to Texas and Washington to Florida. Their native range encompasses major rivers in the Mississippi, Ohio, and Missouri basins. Blues have been introduced in Washington, Oregon, California, Arizona, Colorado, Maryland, Virginia, South Carolina, and Florida.

Blue cats are scarce at the fringes of their range. In many rivers and reservoirs in the South and Midwest, however, ten- to fifty-pounders are as common as two- to five-pound largemouths, and blues to 100 pounds surface with astounding regularity.

Habitat

Blue catfish were originally fish of our big rivers, spending their lives in deep, swift channels and flowing pools. Today, large specimens frequently inhabit the fast-moving tailwaters below dams, where they feed on abundant baitfish like shad and herring. Many also thrive in the open waters of large man-made reservoirs. Although sometimes stocked in ponds and small lakes, blue cats seldom thrive in these environments unless schools of shad or other baitfish are plentiful.

Basic Fishing Tactics

When targeting blue cats, remember they are active year-round. Most catfish fans fish during warm months, but many are learning the blue cat's proclivity for gathering in large winter feeding schools. Each school may contain several trophy-class fish holding near deep, well-oxygenated bottom structures. A quality sonar unit is essential for finding them.

You also should understand that blue cat behavior differs considerably from that of channel and flathead catfish. In fact, in many respects, blue cats behave more like striped bass than other catfish. Shad, herring, and other schooling baitfish comprise most of their diet, and like stripers, blue cats are migratory, following baitfish from area to area. To catch them, you, too, must follow the schools.

Dam tailwaters are among the best river fishing areas. Position yourself a short but safe distance below the dam, and cast your rig into the rushing discharge. Let it sink, then gently pick the weight up, letting the current wash it downstream a few feet. Let the weight down again, and repeat the process. Doing this, you can cover most of the bottom, and cats have a chance to detect the bait and take it.

When fishing outside tailwaters, look for river blues holding near deep, open-water structures.

Anglers targeting trophy blue cats must use sturdy tackle to subdue these hard-fighting heavyweights.

The edges of river channel drop-offs produce many trophy fish, as do deep holes at the confluence of two streams, deep edges of gravel bars, undercut banks near outside bends, and fast deep-water chutes around islands. Blues in lakes usually follow shad schools or can be found near bottom channels, humps, and deep holes.

Stout tackle is a must for subduing trophy-class blues. Rods should be eight- to twelve-foot heavy-action models. Reels, whether level-winding or spinning, should have drags

in good working order. Hooks should be no smaller than 5/0 to 9/0, and you'll need plenty of sinkers to hold your bait on the bottom. Use top-quality line, thirty- to one-hundred-pound-test.

Small blues will eat any of the baits used for channel catfish, but shad and herring are the baits of choice for trophy-class fish. You can use them live or dead, whole, or cut into fillets or chunks.

An egg-sinker rig works fine in most situations. Run the sinker up your main line, and tie a sturdy barrel swivel below it. To the other eye of the swivel tie a twenty-four-inch leader to which you've tied a hook. Impale a baitfish or piece of baitfish on the hook, leaving the point of the hook exposed.

If your hook strikes home, prepare for action. A sizeable blue cat can strip a hundred yards of line before you ever turn its head, but if you can keep the fish away from cover and play it properly, you may with any luck eventually subdue it.

Drift-Fishing

Drift-fishing is the ideal technique for catching hot-weather blue cats on the move.

Blue catfish tend to be nomadic in the summer, moving here and there as they follow schools of baitfish and seek comfort zones in their home waters. They're scattered and difficult to pinpoint, a fact that frustrates many anglers.

In many respects, the behavior of these fish parallels that of striped bass. Like stripers, blues feed almost exclusively on shad, herring, and other schooling baitfish. Consequently they tend to be more migratory than other cats and are more frequently found in open-water habitats. You can sit on the bank and try to catch a mess, but it's not likely to happen. If you try drift-fishing, on the other hand, you may catch dozens of blue cats in a few hours. This is an active approach to catfishing that can make your catch rate soar.

Drift-fishing is just what the name implies. You drift in your boat using the wind, current, or a trolling motor for propulsion. With one or more baited lines out, you keep on the move so you cover more water and increase your odds of crossing paths with a blue cat. Here's some information on this underused catfishing tactic from two experts in the field.

Santee-Cooper Tactics

Joe Drose, a catfishing guide from Cross, South Carolina, often uses drift-fishing to find the big blues inhabiting Marion and Moultrie, the Santee-Cooper lakes.

"Drift-fishing is the only reliable method for catching summer blue cats here," says Drose. "In fact, it's the best way to catch blues throughout most of the year. In spring, we anchor and fish certain spots in the shallows. The blues come shallow then and are more schooled up. The rest of the year, blues roam around and are scattered. Drift-fishing allows you to cover more water so you can find them. If you want to catch blues, you've got to take your bait to them. You can't wait for them to come to your bait."

Some fishermen drift blind. In other words, they have no idea what type of structures or cover is beneath the water. They simply start drifting and hope their hit-and-miss tactics produce more hits than misses. Drose prefers to watch a sonar fish-finder as he drifts with the wind or moves with a trolling motor guiding his boat over and along structures where blue cats are likely to be. Blues may be roaming around, he says, but they'll still do most of their roaming around bottom channels, humps, and other bottom features.

"Most of the time, we're moving back and forth over underwater hills or ridges, moving the bait from twenty to forty feet of water and back," he says. "You never know for sure where the cats will be. Some days you catch most fish in shallower water. Some days most are in deeper water. Some days you'll catch them shallow and deep. That's the thing with summer blues. They're moving all the time. You never know what to expect. That's why drift-fishing works best."

Drose uses one rig—a float rig—when drifting.

"The main line is run through the eye of a 1-1/4- to 1-3/4-ounce pencil weight," he says, "and a barrel swivel is tied below it to keep the weight from sliding down. A four-foot leader is then tied to the lower eye of the swivel. A 2-1/2-inch crappie float is added in the middle of the leader, and a 3/0 or 4/0 wide-bend Eagle Claw hook is tied at the end.

"The float suspends the baited hook above the bottom to help prevent snags," he continues. "By sliding the float up or down the leader, you can adjust the depth at which the bait floats depending on what the catfish are doing. The

Santee-Cooper catfish guide Joe Drose displays a nice blue cat taken while drift-fishing on Lake Marion. Note the drift-fishing rigs in the background.

bait we use is four- to five-inch whole blueback herring."

Drose has caught blue cats up to seventy pounds when drifting and says it's common to catch trophy-class fish—thirty pounds and heavier—using this method. He drifts with one-hundred yards of twenty-five-pound-test line out to keep his rig moving smoothly across the bottom. With lesser lengths of line running behind the boat, the weight has a tendency to drag or snag causing the bait to jump and move wildly about. Four seven- to eight-foot Shakespeare Tiger rods held in rail-mounted rod holders are used for each drift. Each is outfitted with a Shakespeare Tidewater reel that holds up to three hundred yards of twenty-five-pound-test line.

"A high-capacity reel is a must," Drose notes. "If you have one-hundred yards of line out and

A sea anchor helps maintain proper boat speed when drifting big waters under prime weather conditions.

a big blue hits, you better have plenty of line still on the reel, or you could get spooled."

Drose fishes from a large party barge. To slow his drift, he employs one or two custom-made sea anchors (drift socks), each six feet in diameter and attached to the boat with short lengths of nylon rope. The wind pushes the craft along, while the sea anchors govern the drift to a proper speed.

"The best time for drift-fishing is when the water's white-capping some," he says. "You've got to have the sea anchors to control your speed, or you'll go too fast. The anchors also help hold your boat straight so you have a controlled drift and not just a bouncy boat ride."

Jim Moyer's Advice

Jim Moyer of Clarksville, Tennessee, was a long-time catfish guide on Tennessee's Cumberland River and fishes for blue cats on prime waters throughout the country. He agrees with Drose that drift-fishing is one of the best ways for catching scattered summer fish.

"Drift-fishing allows you to cover a lot of water in a short time," says Moyer. "You can cover great distances and cover any depth under controlled conditions. It allows you to present a bait at a specific target or a specific depth. It permits you to target fish from the surface to the bottom. It's very effective in lakes using wind current as your propulsion or in rivers where you're propelled by current."

On the snag-infested waters of Santee-Cooper, Joe Drose must confine his drift-fishing to daylight hours. Moyer, on the other hand, does much of his catfishing on big rivers or open lakes where night fishing often is preferable.

"A lot of times drift-fishing on lakes is at its peak at night because catfish are more active then," he says. "In a river, you can target the fish either in daylight or darkness, but again, the dark hours are best most of the time."

Moyer's technique is very similar to Drose's. On lakes, he drifts with the wind using a trolling motor for direction control and a drift sock to control his speed. In rivers, current carries him along, and a trolling motor keeps him on the right path. A drift sock may be used here again to slow and control the drift.

"Using a trolling motor and a depth-finder," he says, "you can drift along the contours of a river drop-off or other structures where blue cats are likely to be. If you're drifting on a river and the water is high, shallow flats and rocky banks should be your major targets."

Moyer notes, too, that drift-fishing is not limited to a boat. "Baits can be drifted from the bank just as effectively," he says. "Just cast upwind and let the wind or current move your bait into the strike zone. The beauty of this is that a bait can be put in the water a distance away from the target and floated into the strike zone very quietly."

When in a boat, Moyer carries buoys with him to mark locations where fish are hooked. This allows him to drift back through an area again to determine if more cats are present.

"If you catch another fish after your buoy is out, then it's a good idea to anchor and fish the area thoroughly," he says. "When the fish quit biting, retrieve your anchor and buoy and continue to drift."

Moyer offers these tips on proper gear.

Boat: "The type of boat is very important. Boats with high sides are normally harder to drift than boats with low sides."

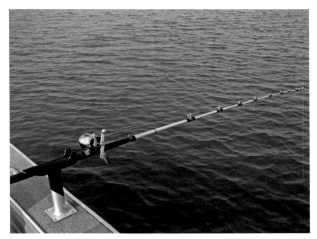

High-capacity reels, long sturdy rods, and quality rod holders firmly mounted on the rails improve the angler's odds of hooking and landing a trophy cat while drift-fishing.

Rods: "Your rod should be seven to seven-and-a-half feet long with a fairly heavy action."

Reels: "A bait-casting reel with a bait runner function is preferable over a spinning reel. The reel should have a fairly large line capacity and an extremely good drag system."

Rod holders: "Rod holders are a must. A twenty-five- or ninety-degree rod holder works best. The rod holder should be designed so the butt of the rod sits deep in the holder but can be easily removed."

Line: "Line should be fairly heavy because of snags and other obstacles encountered while fishing."

Floats: "Floats should be large enough to support the bait and sinker but shaped to create very little resistance in the water when a fish pulls one down. Adjustable floats work better than floats designed to be fixed to the line."

Sinkers: "Sinkers vary as to the type of drifting you are doing. The sinker should be just heavy enough to hold your bait at the depth that you desire."

Hooks: "Hook size is a preference of the fisherman based on the size and type of bait being used. I prefer a minimum of an 8/0 hook. I also find that treble hooks don't work well in drifting situations because they hang more easily."

Three basic rigs comprise Moyer's drift-fishing arsenal.

The drift rig—used for floating live, cut, or dead baits at controlled depths—has a hook, barrel swivel, and sinker configuration from the line's end up. This rig can be tight lined, or a float can be added above the sinker and adjusted on the line so the bait drifts at a preferred depth. In most cases, this rig does not work well in fast drifting situations.

The bottom-bouncing rig—used for a vertical presentation—allows the angler to maintain his "feel" of the bottom when drifting along drop-offs or other structures. A bank sinker is tied to the line's end. A leader to which the hook is tied is positioned on the line above the sinker to hold the bait up off the bottom. When using this rig, the rod should be hand held.

Drifting with multiple poles set at different depths can help anglers determine at what depth catfish in a river are feeding.

When fast drifting baits across the bottom of a river or lake, Moyer considers the bait-walker rig to be the most dependable. Used with cut-bait or dead bait, this rig consists of a one- to three-ounce bait-walker sinker tied to the line with a two- to six-foot hooked leader tied to the sinker's top eye.

"Before you start drift-fishing," says Moyer, "study the area of the lake or river you're planning to fish. Know something about the water depth, structure, water clarity, wind speed, and water speed. Set your rigs at various depths, and let the fish tell you where and how they want the bait.

"Remember what your rig was doing when you caught the fish," he adds. "The first fish could be an accident. The second one could be luck. The third one tells me that the fish are there and are wanting the bait in the same manner.

"Remember, too, that catfish are opportunists, and feed from the surface to the bottom. Use your electronics to help you find the fish, but don't depend totally on this gear because when you're drift-fishing, you're targeting active fish. Just because you don't pick up fish on your initial drift doesn't mean they're not there.

"And finally, because you're targeting active fish, you can expect to catch great numbers when drifting. Twenty or more fish a day are not uncommon."

The key word when drift-fishing, as with any form of catfishing, is experiment. Try to figure out how catfish are likely to react in the type of water you're fishing, then adapt your tactics to conform with those expectations. But if your game plan doesn't produce within a short time, try something different. Sooner or later the innovative cat man discovers a pattern that allows him to capitalize on the situation.

Drift-Fishing Tips

Drift-fishing isn't all luck. Here are tips to improve your success.

A properly set drag reduces the chance of a trophy cat breaking the drifting angler's line.

If you can do so without losing the fish, mark your line when you set the hook in a cat before you reel it in.
This allows you to drift again at the same depth where the first fish was caught, improving your chance of catching another. Release line until you see your mark, and you're back in the strike zone.

- It's important to know how much line you have out when a catfish hits. After you set the hook, mark the line just in front of your reel using a waterproof felt marker. When you release line to that mark and drift through the area again, you know your bait will be at the same depth as before.

- Be sure to properly set your drag.

- Clamp-on rod holders fitted around the transom work OK in some situations, but it's better to use permanently mounted models that won't be torn off when a big cat hits.

- The number of lines you can drift with effectively depends in some degree on the experience of the angler. Experts can sometimes handle four or five rods, but most beginners should start with no more than two. Check local regulations for restrictions.

- How much line should you have out when trolling? The ideal distance varies with water clarity, speed, bait type, and other factors. Experiment to see what works best.

- Let the fish and the motion of the boat do the hooksetting. Wait until the rod has a definite bend in it, then remove it from the holder and boat the fish. Don't stop the trolling motor. Before you get the first fish off, another may be on.

- Watch the birds. Gulls, terns, and other birds will often feed on schools of shad and other baitfish being driven to the surface by white bass, largemouths, stripers, etc. Blue cats will often be under this type of action feeding on crippled bait drifting to the bottom.

Winterkill Patterns

When cold-stressed shad start dying, blue cats begin their annual feeding frenzy.

The big blue cat cruised the lake bottom beneath an enormous school of shad. The water was cold, nearly forty-five degrees, but the catfish was anything but lethargic. He moved rapidly, gorging on scores of baitfish that had become stressed by the low water temperature.

Most of the shad still swam together in a tightly packed school that offered some individual protection from the heavyweight predator and others of his kin. But now and then, a shad succumbed to the icy temperature and swam erratically away from the cluster. Before it swam far, it was wolfed down by the ravenous catfish.

Savvy anglers know that winterkill periods are among the best times for targeting trophy-class blues.

Sitting in a boat above, a man studied a sonar unit and watched as this catfish and others like it cruised the lake bottom. The cats showed up as little animated pixel fish moving across the unit's screen. The shad school appeared as a broad band of black nearly three feet thick. The school was suspended at twenty feet in thirty-five feet of water, too deep to be seen with the naked eye. But now and then, a cold-crippled shad would make its way to the surface, and the fisherman would glimpse its silvery form as it did its death dance in the waning January light.

The man had thrown a cast net across another school of shad thirty minutes earlier near the boat ramp. A dozen live threadfins thus captured had been placed in a round aerated bait tank, and two dozen more were thrown atop the ice in his cooler. With a dip net, the fisherman snatched up a live one, hooked it behind the dorsal fin, and free-spooled his rig to the bottom. He turned the reel handle two revolutions to bring the baitfish up just above the lake bed then placed the rod in a holder affixed to the transom.

As the man was baiting a second rig, the first rod went down. The angler lifted the rod, then without setting the hook, he turned the handle. The circle hook he used required no setting. It caught cleanly in the corner of the big cat's mouth.

During the fifteen-minute battle that ensued, the man forgot all about the cold. The catfish surged straight away at first then began spinning, wrapping itself in the line. Pulling the catfish sideways through the water made it feel like a behemoth, and though it was actually small on a blue cat scale—twenty-one pounds—the man was proud when he finally brought it aboard.

Another shad was rigged and free-spooled to the bottom. Once again, a catfish hit before a second rig could be baited. It, too, was landed, and during the next hour and a half, another and another and another joined it. None were fifty-pounders as the man had hoped, but all were larger than the biggest largemouth bass a man could dream of catching. He caught five cats in ninety minutes, each weighing between eighteen and twenty-six pounds.

The man was not surprised. Catfishing is like that when winterkill begins.

The scene just described may sound like fantasy, but it's not. I was that angler, and I caught those fish using the tactics described.

I learned about the winterkill phenomenon from Joe Drose, a veteran catfishing guide on South Carolina's Santee-Cooper lakes, Marion and Moultrie. You might think the water in this famous Southeastern catfishing hotspot never gets cold enough to produce a shad kill, but such is not the case.

"We usually see some winterkill in December or January," Joe told me. "As the shad start dying and filtering out of the schools, catfish move in by the hundreds and get under baitfish. They gorge on the crippled shad as they drift down out of the schools, a pattern that may last three to four weeks at a time.

"When the temperature is right and this is happening," he continued, "a catfisherman should ride around in his boat and watch his sonar until he finds a big school of baitfish. He then takes a cast net and throws it over the school to collect his bait. The smaller shad seem to work best—those about an inch or two long. Hook two or three at a time on a single hook, running the hook through the eyes and leaving the barb exposed. Then lower your rig all the way to the bottom, reel it up from the bottom about a foot, and get ready for the action that's likely to follow.

"When the catfish are really gorging on shad, you can't use more than one rod per man because they're biting so fast. You drop a bait down and reel it up a little, and before you set the rod in the holder, you'll have a big one on. The action really heats up, and all of a sudden you remember why you're out there fishing on such a cold day. There's nothing more fun and exciting."

On the January day when Joe described this to me, the weather was unseasonably mild, and winterkill had not yet begun. I listened attentively, however, and was eager to learn more when I returned home. Before applying Joe's lesson, I studied the phenomenon. This is what I learned in books and later on the water.

The Reason for Winterkill

Gizzard and threadfin shad are among the most common and widely distributed baitfish in North America. They are mainstays in the diet of blue cats wherever blues and shad are found together. Like striped bass, blues follow shad schools year-round, moving from one spot to another, usually in open-water environments, as they dog their prey.

Both gizzard shad and threadfins are intolerant of severe cold. If the temperature dips below forty-five degrees Fahrenheit in waters where they live, they become cold-stressed. If the cold persists and the water temperature continues

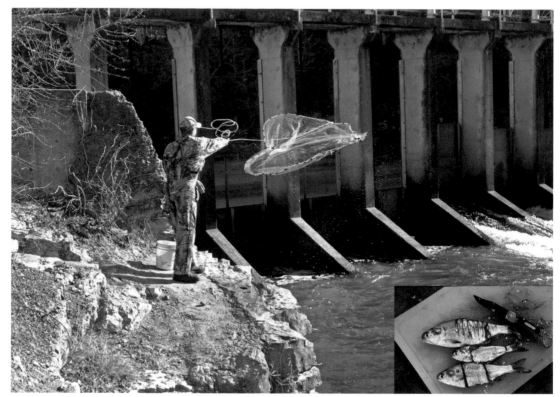

Above: A cast net provides the best means for gathering fresh shad baits to use during winterkill periods. **Inset:** Shad baits can be scored, filleted, or cut in chunks. If one preparation doesn't work, try another, and be sure to use only freshly killed baitfish.

dropping, thousands of shad soon die. This phenomenon, a yearly event on many first-rate blue cat waters, is known in many areas as "winterkill." Some call it "coldkill."

Blue cats feed continuously throughout winter, and when winterkill starts, they flock around shad schools like buzzards around roadkill. Dying baitfish that flutter down through the water column are quickly inhaled by waiting cats one after another after another until the die-off has passed and the catfish are gorged. The pattern may last a day or a month depending on the weather. But while it lasts, fishing for big blues is at its best. Savvy catfishermen capitalize on this cold-weather pattern.

Obtaining and Preparing Shad Baits

The first order of business for winterkill anglers is obtaining shad for bait. At times this is simple; just use a dip net to scoop dead and dying shad from the water, then use them whole or as cutbait. The baitfish should be fresh and will attract more cats if you keep them on ice until you need them.

A cast net is the most effective way to catch live shad, but be sure to check local regulations for restrictions. You can pinpoint the baitfish using sonar, then throw your net over the school, or you can throw a cast net "blind" near shore in areas of well-oxygenated water where shad tend to gather. At times, shad can be seen

a

b

a). The balloon rig used when fishing lakes is very simple. But balloon fishing is most productive if the angler uses sonar to pinpoint schools of shad with larger fish beneath them. Sometimes the big fish prove to be striped bass, but often as not, they're blue cats looking for easy meals. **b).** The author's float rig used when fishing a tailwater.

breaking the water's surface, and the fisherman can move in close and throw a net over the school that has thus been sighted.

If you have a round aerated bait tank that holds at least twenty to thirty gallons of water, you might want to try keeping the shad alive during the entire time you are fishing. A live wiggling baitfish will sometimes outperform cutbait, especially in clear waters, where catfish use sight to locate food. In most situations, however, whole dead shad or shad sliced for cutbait are just as effective as live ones as long as you use baits that were freshly killed. Some anglers prefer to fillet the baits and use strips of the side meat. Others prefer cutting each fish crosswise into sections—head and tail or head, middle, and tail—and use the resulting chunks. Still others use only the guts, "shad gizzards" as they're often called.

I prefer using small shad (those up to three or four inches long) whole, but I score the sides of each bait to release cat-attracting juices into the water. If only a few larger shad are caught, I cut each into three pieces—head, middle, and tail—and I always start by using the middle or "gut" section. Shad guts definitely attract more blue cats than the flesh alone. When I am able to catch dozens of large shad, I use the guts alone, reserving the other parts for use when my bait supply runs low.

Tailwater Tactics

Dam tailwaters serve up some of the best big-river fishing during winterkill periods. Shad that die above a dam drift through the turbines or open gates, and many are sliced and diced in the process. Big blue cats are attracted by the resulting "chum" and often stack up like cord-wood in the tailwater, gorging on the easily gotten pieces of shad that float to them.

In this situation, I prefer a float-rig presentation, so the shad bait drifts through catfish holding areas in much the same way as it would if drifting naturally in the current. The simplest such rig consists of nothing more than a fixed bobber above a hook and perhaps a split shot or two. A more versatile version employs a large sliding bobber. I prefer a three-inch foam egg-shaped model that is brightly colored on top. A bobber stop and plastic bead are placed on the line so the sliding bobber just beneath them will suspend the bait at the desired depth. I usually start by fishing the bait only two feet beneath the surface then move progressively deeper after every five casts until catfish are found. Beneath the bobber, tie an 8/0 to 12/0 circle hook or octopus hook, then if necessary, add several split shot to sink the bait.

Cast this rig as close as possible to the face of the dam, and allow it to drift with the current. I prefer using a twelve-foot surf rod/spinning reel combo, which allows longer casts and permits me to maneuver the rig so it drifts through different areas where blue cats might

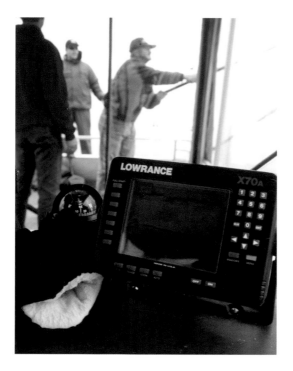

be holding. I find it particularly effective to bring the rig into the slower-moving water in the "grooves" between the dam gates. The bait will often stop momentarily in these spots, and if the winterkill bite is peaking, a blue cat is sure to strike when it does. Other tailwater fishing hotspots include eddy holes (whirlpools) at the end of rock wing dikes, areas of reduced current beside and behind boulders, and along the upstream edge of scour holes created by the churning water releases.

Balloon Fishing in Lakes

I first experienced balloon fishing while fishing for winter striped bass in a large reservoir. My guide used sonar to pinpoint schools of shad with striped bass holding beneath them.

He then positioned the boat over the school of baitfish and used a balloon rig to present the bait to the stripers waiting below.

A live shad was placed on a single wide-gap hook with the hook point piercing it through the eyes. Above the shad, the guide tied a balloon. This was nothing more than a regular round party balloon that was cinched to the line with a tight overhand knot after being inflated to the size of a baseball. The balloon was pushed up so its position on the fishing line was the same as the depth the big fish were holding. The guide then slid the entire rig into the water and let the breeze blow the balloon out over the school of fish.

"We use a balloon on the line because when a fish hits, you can reel it right in," the guide explained. "The balloon will slip off the line when it hits your rod tip without causing any problems."

The tactic worked on stripers, and it works just as well on blue cats. Identify a school of shad on sonar, then look for bigger fish holding below it. These could be striped bass if they are present in the lake you're fishing, but blue cats follow shad schools, too. They often suspend beneath the school, waiting for cold-shocked bait to drift down in the water column. Two or three small shad (live or dead) impaled through the eyes on an 8/0 Kahle hook have proven most effective for me in this situation. When shad were unavailable, I've also used three- to four-inch shiner minnows with success. It's best to use no sinker. This allows the bait to flutter down naturally just like a dead or crippled shad. Blues waiting below can't resist.

Cast Net Info

The cast nets used to collect shad are sized in feet. For example, a six-foot cast net has a radius of approximately six feet. When thrown, it opens into a circle twelve feet in diameter. The thing to remember is that larger cast nets are more difficult to throw. They will, however, catch more shad with each throw. A five- or six-footer with three-eighths-inch mesh usually works well for the weekend angler.

Throwing a cast net properly requires lots of practice. First, tie the retrieving line to your wrist, and with the same hand, grasp the net where it is attached to the line. Hold the weighted line with the other hand and your teeth. Then, twisting like a discus thrower, hoist the net into the water. The net should open into a big circle so the weights pull it down to surround the fish. Then pull the line to draw the net shut and retrieve the baitfish.

Chasing Flatheads

Facts About Flathead Catfish

These fast-growing, cover-loving catfish can be persnickety and hard to catch, but many anglers target them because they're among the most delectable of all freshwater fishes and often grow to huge sizes.

The flathead catfish's scientific name, *Pylodictis olivaris*, comes from Greek and Latin words meaning olive-colored mud fish. That's not a very flattering moniker, but it's a truthful one, for the usually olive-colored flathead often lays on the muddy bottom of a river or lake as it waits to ambush its prey, and that is where it usually is caught by anglers who tempt it with lively fish baits. North America's other big catfish, the channel cat and blue cat, belong to the genus *Ictalurus*. But flatheads differ so much in their physical characteristics that they have been placed in the genus *Pylodictis*, to which no other fish belongs.

Description

The flathead is aptly named, as it has a wide, flattened head unlike other North American catfish. Individual fish may differ in color from others in the same population, ranging from mustard yellow to dark brown or black. In most

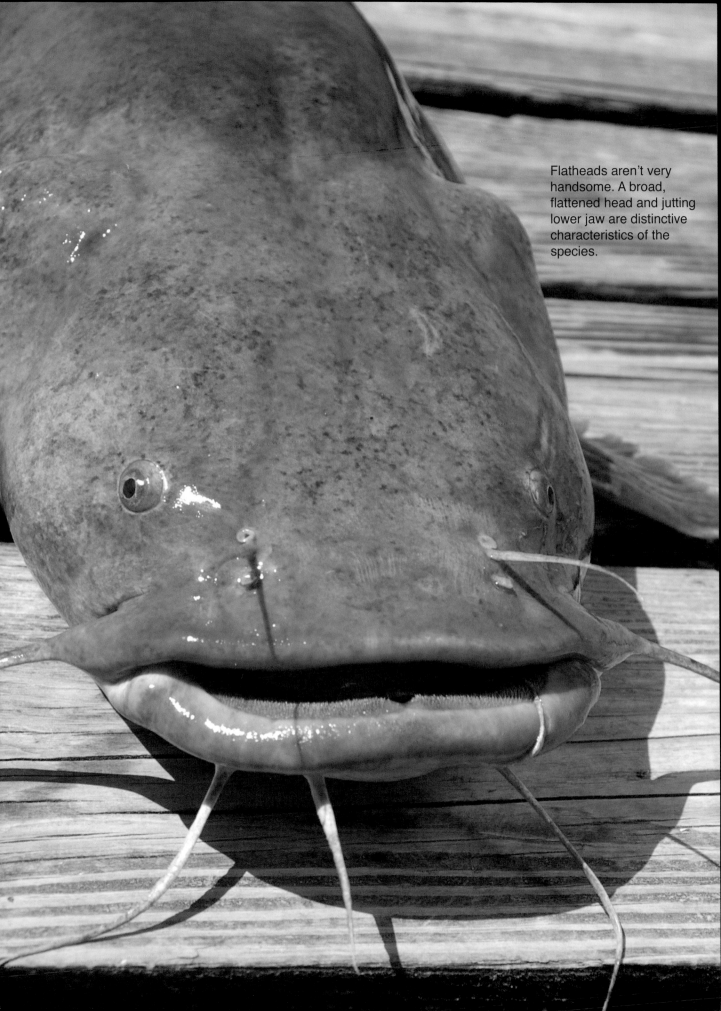

Flatheads aren't very handsome. A broad, flattened head and jutting lower jaw are distinctive characteristics of the species.

Flathead catfish

waters, however, the typical flathead is olive-green to yellowish-brown, often with darker mottling. The belly is pale yellow to cream-white. The tail does not have a deep fork like the tails of channel and blue catfish but is only slightly notched. The flathead also has a distinct underbite—its lower jaw sticks out farther than the upper jaw—which helps distinguish it from other catfish. Small flatheads often resemble bullheads, but the two are easily separated by examining the tooth pad on the upper jaw. On flatheads, this pad has a crescent-shaped backward

extension on each side. Bullheads lack these extensions. Their tooth pads are rounded.

Size

On prime waters during prime times, it's not unusual to catch a dozen or more one- to five-pound flatheads in a few hours of fishing. But flatheads don't stay that small very long. When they reach three years of age, they begin a major growth spurt, commonly adding two to five pounds per year through age eight. After that, they continue packing on the pounds but at an even greater rate. Tag returns indicate older fish may add up to ten pounds annually in some Southern waters.

In lakes and rivers with plentiful forage and good habitat, flatheads exceeding fifty pounds are commonly caught. Of the thirty-three states that list state-record flatheads, 23 have records exceeding 70 pounds. The all-tackle world record is a 123-pounder caught in Kansas' Elk City Reservoir, but flatheads weighing almost seventeen pounds more have been caught using commercial fishing tackle, indicating the possibility that a new world-record flathead might someday be caught on rod and reel.

Food Habits

Studies show that flatheads up to two feet long subsist primarily on a diet of invertebrates, mostly crayfish when they are available. Flatheads greater than two feet long eat mostly fish, including shad, sunfish, suckers, and other catfish.

Unlike channel cats and blues, flatheads rarely scavenge, preferring live foods over dead. Baits such as chicken liver, commercial stinkbaits, or cutbaits that frequently are used for tempting channel cats and small blues sometimes entice small flatheads. But for consistent success, savvy flathead anglers use live fish for bait and nothing else.

Individual flatheads may vary greatly in coloration.

Adult flatheads feed primarily on live fish, and, thus, live fish baits are most likely to catch them.

In temperate climes, flatheads feed year-round, but feeding ceases when they are spawning, and they feed little or none when the water temperature falls below about forty-five degrees Fahrenheit. They are rarely caught in winter unlike blue and channel catfish.

Range

The flathead's original range encompassed much of the Mississippi, Mobile, and Rio Grande river drainages and the Great Lakes region in mid-America from North Dakota to Texas in the West and from Pennsylvania to Alabama in the East. Introductions have expanded the species' range to parts of Arizona, California, Colorado, Florida, Georgia, Idaho, Oregon, Pennsylvania, North Carolina, South Carolina, Virginia, Washington, and Wyoming, as well.

Habitat

Flathead catfish seldom exist in large numbers in small bodies of water, like ponds and creeks. However, they are well adapted to life in rivers, larger man-made reservoirs, and many natural lakes where thriving populations often produce excellent fishing opportunities. In rivers, they generally avoid heavy current but sometimes feed in swift water at the ends of dikes and in tailraces below dams.

When looking for flatheads during daylight hours, focus your attention on areas with dense woody cover. These predators often hide around or within submerged logs, piles of driftwood, toppled trees, snags, and cavities in mid-depths, waiting to ambush passing prey. At night, they leave these sanctuaries and move into more open, shallow waters to feed. Adults tend to be solitary and often are aggressive toward others of their kind. Thus, a single spot of cover usually yields only one or at most two or three adult flatheads.

Basic Fishing Tactics

In rivers, look for flatheads in areas with a steady water flow and hardened mud or gravel bottom. The outside bends of rivers are among the most productive hotspots, especially where

Big flatheads are cover lovers, often found buried in treetops, log jams, and other woody cover from which they ambush their prey.

trees have toppled into the water and the river has gouged deeply into the bank, forming undercuts. Potholes or slight depressions in the river bottom also tend to concentrate flatheads, as do the upstream sides of underwater humps, shallow flats and drops near tributary mouths, and the whitewater tailraces below big dams.

Reservoir flatheads usually seek cover near areas of fast-breaking structure. A sonar unit can help locate flatheads holding on or near stream channels meandering across the bottom. Inundated ponds are honeyholes because they offer flatheads easy access to both deep-water holding areas and shallow feeding spots. Other areas to investigate include current-breaking cover where streams feed the lake, sloping points near the junctions of inundated channels, and steep rocky ledges with adjacent timber. Prime

hotspots provide well-oxygenated water, plenty of cover and food, and some current.

When trophy fish are targeted, heavy tackle is a must. Most ardent flatheaders favor heavy-action rods eight to twelve feet long, big level-wind reels, and thirty- to fifty-pound line. The baitfish is hooked through the eyes, nose, or back using a 5/0 to 8/0 hook tied below an egg sinker heavy enough to hold the rig on the bottom. More complicated rigs can be used, but this simple version works fine for most situations.

When fishing from a boat, lower the rig straight down into the spot you've selected and leave your reel in free-spool while you wait for a cat to take the bait. Bank fishermen can hold their rod or place it in a firmly anchored rod holder. Leave the reel in free-spool until you detect a strike, and always be sure your reel's drag is properly set.

High-Rise Flatheads

Flood-stage rivers and lakes can be fished if you employ the right tackle and techniques.

Flathead catfish differ from other cats in many ways. For example, flatheads aren't very mobile. During a year, they usually roam no more than a mile from the single unit of cover they call home. Blue and channel catfish often travel many miles.

Flatheads also are solitary fish and aggressive to others of their own kind unlike blues and channels, which frequently live in small groups

or loose schools. A prime piece of flathead real estate—usually a log pile or other protected site where woody debris has accumulated—rarely contains more than one adult fish.

I mention these two characteristics in particular because they affect the catch rates of many catfishermen, especially those of us who enjoy fishing from shore. If you fish primarily from the bank and not a boat, you must depend on the enticing movement, taste, and smell of a live baitfish—the best flathead attractor—to draw your quarry in. The problem is that flatheads don't move much, and when they do, they roam alone. An angler working a pool from the bank is lucky to catch one decent flathead during several nights of fishing.

Spring Spree

There is a time, however, when flatheads abandon these typical patterns. In spring, when heavy rains cause rivers and lakes to rise and become muddy, flatheads go on a run-and-gun feeding spree. Some anglers believe they are hungry after a winter on lean rations, and the sudden influx of food animals washed into the water by warm rain stimulates feeding activity. Others believe the spawning urge draws the fish together, and they feed ravenously to fatten up before the austerity of egg laying and nesting. Whatever the case, this is a

Flatheads feed ravenously during high water periods in spring, making this one of the best times for multiple hookups with big fish.

boon time for flathead fans. No better situation exists for catching flatheads in numbers.

My best night fishing for flatheads was on the lower Mississippi River in April under conditions such as those I just described. The river was well above flood stage and muddy enough to track a coon across. Fishing a steep, timbered bank of revetment, two friends and I boated more than 150 flatheads that weighed two to twenty-five pounds.

Nights such as that are unusual even in high water, but if you use proper techniques, highrise flatheads will provide exciting action. Safety considerations must be foremost on your mind, of course. And for that reason, bank fishing is actually the best choice in this situation. I prefer fishing the points on both sides of a tributary mouth, where I can work a broad swath of water, but areas above and below log jams, wing dikes, and bridges also have proven productive.

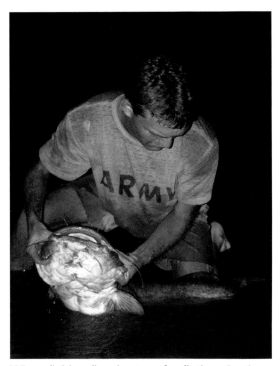

When fishing floodwaters for flatheads, the bank fisherman often finds himself battling a big cat in extremely shallow water.

Hands-on Fishing

Leave your rod holders home. This is active fishing with the rod in your hand. I work the bait one to two feet beneath an orange-sized

Few anglers target catfish during spring floods because fast-moving waters can be dangerous and make fishing difficult. Nevertheless, this is one of the best periods for finding flatheads on the move, as they gorge on the abundance of food brought into the water by rain.

float (high-rise flatheads seldom feed deep), casting it upstream as far as possible then allowing the rig to drift on a fairly tight line. When my rig nears the end of each drift, before it gets snagged near the bank downstream, I reel in, cast upstream again, and repeat the

process. I work from far to near (in relation to the bank) on successive casts.

Because huge flatheads are possible, maybe even a one-hundred-pounder, I use large sturdy hooks, stout line, and a tough rod-and-reel combo. Favored tackle consists of a ten- to twelve-foot surf rod for increased casting distance and better rig control, a heavy spinning reel spooled with fifty- to eighty-pound-test braided line, and an 8/0 to 12/0 circle hook. I prefer a simple more snag-free rig with no weight other than the bait itself due to the large amount of floating debris in the water. And the bait is not always the live fish (sunfish, carp or bullhead) I prefer during other seasons. In flood waters, flatheads feed more indiscriminately, and I often catch them on crawfish, shad guts, and large balls of big night crawlers in addition to fish. Night fishing always is best.

Other game plans may work as well or better, and like I always say, experimenting is half the fun of catfishing. Try your own rigs and techniques, but be sure you don't miss out on this seasonal catfishing bonanza.

Autumn Angles

Autumn flathead fishing runs a dead heat with spring in terms of action.

There's no doubt that flathead feeding activity increases in October, November or December (depending on the latitude). My catch rate improves as summer's heat dissipates and days grow shorter. And I've spoken to dozens of flathead men who experience the same thing. Why the bite improves is a matter of speculation, but like many cat men, I believe flatheads feed more in autumn because they sense a season on low rations is about to begin.

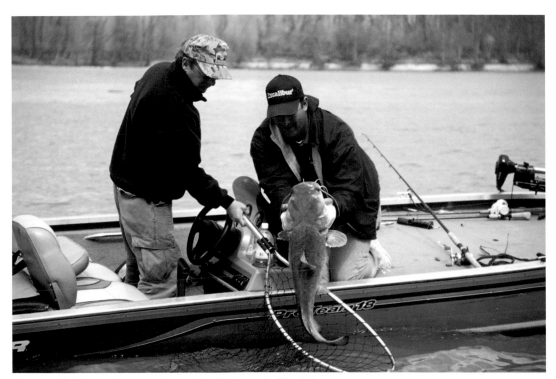

Autumn fishing often produces big flatheads like this.

"Flatheads are like bears," one old-timer told me. "They have to fatten up in fall because they're gonna hibernate till spring. That's why the fall bite is so good." Some dispute that claim, saying flatheads feed actively throughout winter. Maybe in some places, they do. They don't where I fish, however, and I don't know a single flathead man who actively pursues his quarry when the water temperature drops below the mid-forties. There's just not enough feeding activity to justify the effort.

Hardcore Evidence

Two hardcore divers I know provided additional evidence that flatheads become inactive in cold water. Both men noted they often see flatheads congregated in deep water during winter. Invariably, they say, the flatheads are lying on the bottom, sometimes covered with silt, and the fish are so lethargic the divers can actually touch them without spooking them, something that's impossible during other seasons. The flatheads, they report, appear to be in suspended animation.

All this evidence lends veracity to the old-timer's hibernating bear analogy. There's a distinct peak in flathead feeding in autumn because these fish follow instinctive urges to put on weight before the cold "starvation" period ahead.

The reasons why flatheads go on a feeding binge in fall are not as important as the fact they do. Autumn is prime flathead time, and if you want to waylay a trophy specimen, fish as often as possible until harsh winter cold sets in.

It looks almost impossible to fish—a huge rotating mat of floating logs and debris. But eddy-water log rafts like this are prime spots for targeting autumn flatheads.

Fishing Log Rafts

Eddy-water log rafts are my favorite structures to fish this season. These are mats of floating logs and debris that form in big-river backwaters, usually during high-water periods. As the river's current velocity increases, the moving river water presses against the seam of quieter backwater and causes it to circulate like a giant slow-moving vortex. Logs and other woody debris in the river are sucked into this big eddy and form rafts sometimes several hundred yards across. The rafts attract baitfish and other forage animals, which in turn attract flatheads.

To fish these rafts, secure your boat off to one side or find a bank-fishing spot that allows access to the outer edges of the raft. Flatheads often hold beneath central portions of the raft, but it's much easier to fish the edges where flatheads also feed. Live fish baits work best, as they almost always do for flatheads, and can be presented on a simple egg-sinker rig—a one-ounce egg sinker above a barrel swivel to which your leader and hook are tied. Don't use an overly large sinker. You want the eddy to grab your rig and pull it under the outer edge of the log raft. Use just enough weight to carry the bait slowly to the bottom in whatever current is present. Then, after casting, hold your rod tip high and strip line manually from your reel, guiding your rig beneath the rotating maze of logs. If a bite hasn't come by the time your line is caught by a piece of driftwood, move it and try again. If flatheads are present, they'll usually bite within a few minutes after your bait touches bottom.

Tributaries

Tributary mouths are good places to focus your efforts on lakes. If current flow is good in the in-flowing creek or river, eddy water can be found here, too. And if some type of dense woody cover is present, as well—log rafts, blowdowns, drift piles, etc.—flatheads are likely to be lying in wait.

In this situation, I usually fish a sliding-bobber rig: a bobber stop and big slip bobber above a few split shot and a hook. By moving the bobber stop up or down your line, you can fish different depths easily, and this type of rig can be cast great distances using a long rod. Cast upstream as far as you can in the tributary, then use your rod tip to guide your rig past the woody cover. Make a drift through one area, then if a bite isn't forthcoming, cast and drift through again, moving your bait past different structures. If a fall flathead is in the neighborhood, you'll nail him on one drift or another.

Bullhead Fishing

Facts About Bullhead Catfish

Bullheads don't get very big, but these pugnacious little catfish can provide hours of fun for the panfishing enthusiast.

Because bullheads rarely weigh more than two pounds, many people shun them and focus their fishing efforts on larger species of catfish. Nevertheless, lots of folks love these little cats, because bullheads often are plentiful and always fun to catch. Their scaleless bodies, big-lipped mouths, and long whiskers won't win them any piscatorial beauty contest. But when rolled in seasoned cornmeal and fried golden-brown, bullheads earn a blue-ribbon for scrumptiousness. Their abundance and ready catchability make them perfect targets for kids eager to catch some fish.

Description

Six species of bullheads inhabit North American waters. Three of these—the flat bullhead, snail bullhead, and spotted bullhead—average less than a foot in length and have restricted ranges in small portions of the Southeastern United States. Few people fish for them. We'll focus our attention on the other three

Some anglers frown when they catch a bullhead, detesting this little catfish for its bait-stealing habits and diminutive size. Many, however, prize this bantam brawler, which can provide hours of fun in waters where it is abundant.

species—black, brown, and yellow bullheads—which reach larger sizes, have extensive ranges, and are popular targets of catfish anglers throughout much of the country.

Black bullhead

The black bullhead (*Ameiurus melas*) is a dark, robust, small-eyed catfish with an almost square or slightly notched tail. Adults are a solid brownish yellow to black and have no mottling. The anal fin has seventeen to twenty-one rays. Gray or black chin barbels are present but never white. The pectoral fin spines have weakly developed teeth along the rear edge or no teeth at all.

Brown bullhead

The brown bullhead (*Ameiurus nebulosus*) has light-brown sides that are distinctively mottled with darker markings. The degree of mottling, however, is highly variable. This species is similar to the black bullhead but differs from it in having well-developed teeth on the rear edges of the pectoral spines (versus no teeth or weakly developed teeth) and in having twenty-one to twenty-four anal fin rays (versus seventeen to twenty-one). Unlike the yellow bullhead, its chin barbels are pigmented with gray or black.

Yellow bullhead

The yellow bullhead (*Ameiurus natalis*) closely resembles the brown and black bullheads, with a squat body and a round or square tail, but it differs from these species in having white chin barbels (versus gray or black barbels) and in having twenty-four to twenty-seven anal fin rays (versus having twenty-four or fewer). It differs from blue and channel catfishes in having a straight or rounded margin on its tail versus a forked tail. Adults have a solid yellowish to brownish or black body with no mottling.

Many colorful nicknames are used to describe bullheads. "Horned pout" seems universal, and the nicknames "greaser" and "slick" also are widely used. Other colloquial names include polliwog, polly, paperskin, mudcat, stinger, snapper, butterball, bullcat, and bullpout.

Size

A two-pound bullhead, regardless of species, is considered a big healthy specimen in most waters. Much larger ones are occasionally caught, however. Black bullheads reach the largest maximum size. The all-tackle record weighed eight pounds, fifteen ounces. The brown bullhead record is six pounds, five ounces, and the record yellow bullhead tipped the scales at four pounds, fifteen ounces.

Food Habits

Bullheads eat many types of foods from minnows and crayfish to carrion and insects. "They will take any kind of bait," wrote Henry David

Thoreau, "from angleworms to a piece of tomato can …"

While using a piece of tomato can for bait might be stretching your luck, there's no denying these little cats are not temperamental. You can catch them on everything from bacon and hot dogs to minnows and crayfish. Among the best baits, however, are fresh chicken liver, worms, and stinkbaits.

Range

The black bullhead ranges from southern Canada, the Great Lakes, and the St. Lawrence River south to the Gulf of Mexico and from Montana and New Mexico east to the Appalachians.

The range of the brown bullhead encompasses most of the eastern half of the United States and Southeastern Canada. It also has been widely introduced outside its native range. In parts of New England, the brown bullhead is the only catfish available to anglers.

The yellow bullhead swims in waters throughout the Eastern and Central United States with many transplants elsewhere.

Habitat

Oxbow lakes, river backwaters, pools in small streams, and other areas with quiet, turbid water and a silty bottom are the preferred home waters of black bullheads.

The brown bullhead prefers moderately clear, heavily vegetated streams and lakes.

The yellow bullhead tends to inhabit smaller weedier bodies of water than its cousins and reaches its greatest abundance in areas of dense vegetation in shallow clear bays of lakes, ponds, and slow-moving streams.

Basic Fishing Tactics

You can catch bullheads using the same tactics employed for catching eating-sized channel cats, but you may want to downsize your fishing tackle for these small fish. Small hooks, light line, and ultralight rod-and-reel combos work great.

Bait choices are legion. Bullheads are the fish world's equivalent of barnyard hogs. There's hardly anything they won't eat. Live crayfish, minnows, nightcrawlers, shad, catalpa worms, salamanders, leeches, maggots, tadpoles, or toads will do just fine. Dead stuff such as chicken liver, mussels, shrimp, and fish guts are on the menu, as well. Weird things, too, like dog food, corn, soap, sour grain, hot dogs, marshmallows, bread, cheese, and even bubble gum are acceptable. Indeed, bullheads will engulf anything remotely resembling food, so you'll probably catch one sooner or later no matter what your bait choice.

Those big rubbery lips make bullheads somewhat hard to hook, so always use extra-sharp hooks.

A stringer of fat bullheads provides the makings for a delicious fish dinner.

How to Catch Record-Class Bullheads

Massachusetts catfishing expert Roger Aziz has caught some of the biggest bullheads ever documented. The tips he shares can help you land some monster bulls, too.

Call him The Bullhead King or just plain bullheaded. Either way, Roger Aziz Jr. of Methuen, Massachusetts, will take it as a compliment. Hundreds of thousands of people in this country love bullhead fishing, but no one loves fishing for these pugnacious little catfish more than Roger.

No one knows more about bullhead fishing, either, a fact exemplified by the many record bullheads Roger has caught. Aziz has established International Game Fish Association line-class records for yellow bullheads four times and for brown bullheads twice. The National Fresh Water Fishing Hall of Fame has recognized ten brown bullheads he's caught as line-class and all-tackle records plus five yellow bullhead line-class records.

Roger's biggest bullhead to date was a six-pound, four-ounce yellow bullhead caught May 25, 2008, in the fifty-five-acre Forest Lake in Methuen. Twenty-three inches long with a thirteen-inch girth, that fish was a giant of its kind and is recognized as the current Massachusetts state record. The currently recognized IGFA all-tackle world record is just two ounces heavier. Aziz caught a previous Massachusetts record—a three-and-a-half pound brown bullhead—in 1985. To give you an idea of how hard it is to catch a bullhead even of that size, the record stood more than twenty years before being broken.

While bullhead fishing is one of Roger's specialties, let's not cubbyhole the man into that single niche. Roger is one of the few freshwater fishing guides in Massachusetts with more than

Roger Aziz Jr. shows off the six-pound, four-oun yellow bullhead he caught, which was certified a Massachusetts state record. This is one of the la bullheads ever documented.

twenty-five years experience fishing for a wide variety of sportfish—everything from trout, salmon, and American shad to bass, carp, and saltwater species. "If it has fins, I can catch it," he says. He's also a tournament champion, angling consultant, lecturer, and writer. Make no mistake about it, however, Roger Aziz knows as much about catfishing, and particularly bullhead fishing, as any angler in the world. His tips will prove useful to anyone desiring to catch the biggest bullheads swimming where they fish.

Developing a Game Plan

"I started fishing for bullheads at a very early age," says Aziz, who was born in 1961. "Like sunfish, they seem to show up on your line no matter where you're fishing. Most don't get very big—maybe a pound or two. A three-pound bullhead is quite unusual—equivalent to, let's say, a ten-pound largemouth bass. When I started catching some bullheads that size, I knew I was on to something good. So I began my own research projects to learn more about the way these monster bullheads function."

Although bullheads inhabit a variety of waters, Aziz determined that ponds stocked with trout tend to be home waters for the biggest bulls.

"In New England, trout are stocked in two basic types of ponds: those that are spring fed and those that are not," he says. "Most stocked ponds that are spring fed have a low fish kill rate. Trout thrive in these waters year-round. But ponds that aren't spring fed tend to be eutrophic (rich in nutrients) with little or no trout survival due to oxygen depletion and other factors.

"The eutrophic ponds are best for bigheads," he continues. "Dead trout lay on the bottom of the ponds, and something is going to eat them. Most likely, that something will be bullheads, which often consume carrion. And the more trout the bullheads consume—the more raw protein they eat—the bigger they get."

In spring-fed lakes, natural trout die-offs are rare, but many trout still perish due to angling pressure and mishandling.

"Big bulls become more predator-like in these spring-fed lakes," Aziz says. "But they still can be caught if you use the right tactics."

Tackle

Were you to accompany Aziz on one of his bullhead-fishing junkets, you might be rather amazed at the tackle he uses, much of which is unfamiliar to American anglers.

"I opt to use Euro tackle," he says, "the same stuff our fishing pals from across the pond use for carp fishing. My rods are thirteen feet long with a three-and-three-quarter-pound test curve. By American standards, this is a heavy-action rod with a fast tip, which provides enough loading power that I can catapult a bait rig great distances. My reels are bait-runner reels that allow the line to be pulled out by a fish without an open spool. These are loaded with fifteen-pound-test Berkeley Big Game Solar line tipped with a forty-pound-test fluorocarbon shock leader six feet long."

Aziz fishes with this European-style carp-fishing tackle.

Aziz sometimes fishes from a boat, but because most ponds he fishes at are relatively small, more likely than not you'll find him on shore when he's targeting big bullheads. He fishes with multiple rod/reel combos supported on a Gardner stainless-steel rod pod, a device developed by carp anglers that allows rods to lie horizontally and be tended hands-free. The pod is coupled with Delkim electronic strike alarms that detect the slightest line movement and rod vibrations. When a bullhead bites, these sound an alarm "loud enough to wake anyone from a deep sleep," says Aziz.

When night fishing, Aziz also carries at least three propane lanterns plus head lanterns and flashlights. All his equipment is carried in a Fox rucksack, which resembles a backpack with a four-legged frame to keep equipment stable and off the ground.

On the business end of each fishing line, Aziz ties a tandem bait rig.

"Each rig consists of a No. 2 wide-bend hook followed by a Kahle hook varying in size from 2/0 to 5/0. The hooks are connected to each other by snell knots, all following IGFA rules."

Unlike most catfish anglers, Aziz uses no lead sinkers on his rigs or very small sinkers. His baits—bacon, sunfish, or minnows—are sunk to the bottom with a bar of soap. Yes, soap.

Soaping

Using soap for catfish bait is nothing new (see Chapter 23). But Aziz has carried "soaping," as he calls it, to a whole new level.

"Soaping is a ground-bait technique I conjured myself," he says. "I take a bar of Dial soap, any exotic scent, and drive a homemade eye screw through the whole bar. The soap is part of my fishing rig and acts as both a weight and an

Bars of Dial soap rigged with homemade eye screws serve as weights and bullhead attractors on Aziz's fishing rigs.

attractor. The scent is limited to a radius of a couple of feet in lakes or ponds, but it's a real big bullhead attractant."

A long process of experimentation helped Aziz refine this tactic. He knew catfish rely heavily on scent to help them find food items. But experience showed that scent didn't have to be from something dead and rotten like a trout carcass.

"I figured if I could attract carp with ground bait, a concoction of bread crumbs and other household foods, why not bullheads?" he says. "The ground bait used for carp works OK but dissipates quickly in water. I wanted an attractor that would melt slowly and attract anything swimming by. Soap turned out to be that attractor. I tested a variety of scents to see which would work better, and it turns out they all work very well. I use Dial soap because it's very inexpensive and very heavy. I can cast it long distances, and it sinks quickly to the bottom. It comes in many sweet-smelling fragrances that attract monster bulls."

To prepare the soap for rigging, Aziz takes a six-inch piece of forty-gauge wire and grinds it flat on both ends. Then, using a wire-forming machine, he creates an eye on one end of wire with a long wrap. The wire can then be pushed and screwed into the middle of the soap on one end. The wire wrap below the eye works like a screw to keep the soap secure.

The wired soap is attached to the main line via a swivel on a sliding fish-finder sleeve. The main line runs through the sleeve with the sleeve held in place above the hooks using a small piece of plastic tubing crimped on the line. The hooks are then baited with pieces of bacon, small whole sunfish or minnows, or small pieces of cutbait prepared from the baitfish.

When fishing from shore, this whole rig is cast out, allowed to sink, and sits stationary on the bottom while Aziz waits for a bite. If he is fishing from a boat, however, Aziz's fishing method is a bit diffcrent.

"In a boat, I use a six-foot medium-heavy rod with a fast taper," he says. "I do not attach the soap to my line but instead chum bars of soap over the side of the boat. The area I chum is where I place my bait. I use a sinker that's as light as possible."

It's not a huge fish, but this four-pound, four-ounce brown bullhead caught by Roger Aziz is a giant of its kind. Only rarely do anglers catch bullheads this large.

Seasonal and Locational Information

Aziz doesn't ice-fish for bullheads but targets them whenever the New England ponds he fishes are ice free.

"Spring is when bulls are at their heaviest," he says. "They spawn from the latter part of May through early June and are filled with eggs.

"From the latter part of June through July, big bulls are more difficult to catch. This is the postspawn period when bulls are busy guarding their fry and not feeding heavily.

"From August until November, bullhead fishing can be great as long as the weed growth is light," he continues. "Big ones hold six to twenty feet deep then. I find that the monster bulls usually bolt when accepting the bait in the spring when weed growth is sparse. But in summer, when the weed growth is at its peak, monster bulls stay in their weed patches and don't move much at all. Finding the right weed patch is hard. It takes a lot of trial and error. Bullheads being omnivorous will feed on the weeds they lie in when other forage is not available. And in the weeds, the bite is not bolting and aggressive but subtle. I have to keep my eye on the line whether a bite indicator is used or not. The good thing is, competition from smaller bulls is not as much in weed patches. I usually catch big bulls when fishing these spots."

During the latter part of this period, from late October into November, fishing may be extremely difficult, Aziz notes.

Fish Light

Use ultralight spinning or spincast combos. Four- to eight-pound line is appropriate in all but the most snag-infested waters. Hooks for bullheads range in size from No. 4 to 1/0.

Fish Right at Night

Bullheads feed around the clock, but the night bite usually is best. Bullheads avoid current. Zero in on deep holes in creeks, backwater areas on rivers, weed bed edges in ponds and swamps, boat docks, long points, and underwater humps in lakes.

Keep it Simple

The simpler your fishing methods, the more you will enjoy bullhead fishing. Your strategy can be as unencumbered as using a cane pole and small hook to dunk a worm or piece of liver. Fish on bottom using a small sinker to carry your bait down. Or use a bobber to float the bait slightly above the bottom. You need not fish deep or far from shore.

Hooking What Bites

Bullheads have a propensity for holding the bait, letting the angler reel them in, then spitting the bait out at the last second. When tightlining, let the fish start moving off before you strike. Count to three, then set the hook with a quick upward snap. When bobber fishing, wait until the float disappears or starts moving slowly away. That's usually when the fish has the bait in its mouth.

Carry Plenty of Hooks

Bullheads are notorious hook swallowers, so carry plenty of hooks. You can remove hooks with a disgorger or long-nosed pliers, but it's quicker to cut the line and retrieve hooks when cleaning your catch. Better yet, use small circle hooks, which tend to hook the fish in the corner of the mouth and are easily removed.

Blow up a Worm

Night crawlers are irresistible to bullheads, especially when you use a hypodermic syringe to inflate them. Adding a shot of air in the body lifts the worms up, making them more visible to the fish. Your sinker sits on bottom; your crawlers ride high.

Really Red Worms

Soak worms in red pickled beet juice to make them more attractive to bullheads. This also toughens their "hides," making it harder for bullheads to steal them off the hook.

Soaking night crawlers in beet juice toughens them and makes them more attractive to bullheads.

Bait Options

A trip to the grocery will turn up many superb bullhead baits. Bacon works great, especially hickory-smoked. Chunks of hot dog and cheese are relished, too, and fresh chicken livers can't be beat. Bread and even bubble gum work in a pinch.

Liver Rig

A small treble hook attached to your line with a snap swivel works great when fishing liver. Unsnap the swivel, remove the hook, push the eye of the hook through the liver so the liver is impaled on the three barbs, then reattach the hook to the swivel. The liver is now less likely to fly off when you cast.

Doughbait Recipe

Here's a popular formula for doughbait to entice bullheads. Run a pint of chicken livers through a blender until liquefied. Slowly add Wheaties cereal, and continue blending until the mixture turns into a ball. Roll into grape-sized pieces and place in a zip-seal bag. Cool to firm before using.

Bullhead Turnoffs

Bullheads can detect and will avoid even minute quantities of sunscreen, gas, oil, or insect repellent that come in contact with your bait. Avoid these if possible. If you can't, wear rubber gloves when handling bait.

Don't Get "Horned"

Avoid the bullhead's sharp pectoral and dorsal fin spines. If you get poked, old-timers recommend swiping the fish's belly across the wound to neutralize the stinging sensation. Household ammonia daubed on the wound has the same effect.

No Shadows

Bullheads scurry for cover when a shadow passes overhead. If you fish during daylight hours, you'll have more luck if you place yourself so the sun never casts your shadow on the spot where you are fishing.

A great way to catch bullheads is with fresh chicken liver on a snap-swivel rig.

Caution should be used when handling bullheads, which have extremely sharp spines.

Tie a Break Knot

Bullheads often dash for cover when hooked, causing hang-ups. An overhand knot tied above your hook will help you save your line should the hook become snagged in deep water. A quick jerk will break the line at the knot instead of the rod tip.

Winter Fishing

Some anglers say bullheads won't bite in winter. They're wrong. To enjoy light tackle fun during cold months, head for the nearest bullhead pond and drop a bait in the deepest water you can find. Bullheads often gather in huge concentrations in deep wintering holes, and if you can pinpoint such a place, you'll soon be enjoying fish-a-minute action.

Keep 'em Cold

If you catch bullheads in clean water and ice them down immediately, they're delicious. Fish taken in muddy or polluted water may have a disagreeable taste regardless of how you care for them.

Which Cat is That?

Want to know what kind of bullhead you caught? It's easy to separate the three common species by looking at the chin barbels (whiskers) and fins. Yellow bullheads have whitish or yellowish chin barbels. Brown bullheads have dark chin barbels like black bullheads, but on browns the pectoral fin spines on each side just behind the head have well-developed "teeth" along the rear edge; teeth are absent or weakly developed on the black bullhead's pectoral fin spines.

Cleaning Tips

Always skin bullheads and remove dark red meat along the lateral line. This rids the dressed fish of unsavory flesh. Avoid puncture wounds by snipping off the spines with wire cutters before cleaning your catch. Skinning is easier if you use an ice pick to secure the fish to a board or tree.

A Tasty Recipe

Here's a bullhead recipe that's hard to beat. Combine ¾ cup yellow cornmeal, ¼ cup flour, 2 teaspoons salt, ½ teaspoon cayenne pepper, and ½ teaspoon garlic powder in a large bag. Add fish and shake to coat. Fill a cooker half full of peanut oil and heat to 365 degrees Fahrenheit. Add fish and fry until the fish flakes easily with a fork, about five minutes. Serve piping hot.

Kids' Fish

Because they're abundant and rather easy to catch, bullheads are great kids' fish. Next time you fish for them, take a youngster along. It's a great way to spend a day.

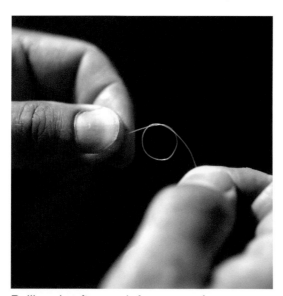

Bullheads often rush for cover when hooked. Tying a simple overhand knot in your line allows you to break it off easier if the fish gets too ensnarled for extraction.

Seasonal Savvy

Understanding the Spawn

There are good reasons your catch rate may fall when cats are spawning.

"The bluegills are bedding!" "The white bass are running!" "Crappie are spawning!" "Largemouths are moving up shallow!"

Spawning season is peak time to catch many gamefish, and when the rally cry is heard, folks flock to the water to enjoy some of the year's best action. The spawning habits of catfish, however, differ greatly from the spawning habits of other gamefish. Catfishing success may take a nosedive when blues, flatheads, and channel cats are on their nests, and unless you understand why this occurs, you're likely to return from a fishing trip frustrated and perplexed.

Spawning Behavior

Our major catfish species spawn during spring or summer when the water warms to an optimal temperature. Channel cats spawn at seventy to eighty-four degrees Fahrenheit, but eighty to eighty-one degrees is considered best. Flatheads spawn at sixty-six to seventy-five degrees. Blue catfish spawning requirements are believed to be similar to those of channel catfish.

The swollen head on this big channel cat indicates it is a male ready to guard a nest full of eggs. While protecting its eggs, it may not feed for days, making it tough to catch.

Spawning begins at different times in different latitudes progressing from south to north. With channel cats, for instance, spawning may begin in March or April in South Carolina or Texas, May in Kansas or Iowa, and mid-June to July in South Dakota or Wyoming. Blue catfish spawn April through June in Louisiana and early July in Iowa. Flatheads spawn in late June in Arkansas but not until weeks later in northern parts of their range.

All our cats are cavity nesters. Blue catfish deposit their eggs between rocks, in root wads, depressions, undercut banks, or other areas protected from current. Flatheads select sites such as hollow logs, excavated caves in clay banks, root masses from downed trees, or manmade structures, such as old tires, car bodies, and metal drums. Channel catfish have been observed to spawn directly on the bottom at sites with no nearby cover, but they usually select dark, secluded spots, such as crevices in piles of woody debris, burrows in banks, and spaces between and under rocks. If suitable spawning habitat is unavailable, catfish may

Catfish are cavity nesters, as the hatchery manager well knows. To provide spawning sites in hatchery ponds, old milk cans are often placed on the bottom where each female catfish can lay her mass of yellow eggs. Male cats then guard the eggs until they hatch.

migrate from a lake into a tributary stream, for example, to find it.

A sexually mature male selects and cleans a nest site and spawns with a female he lures there. After the female lays her mound of sticky yellow eggs, the male fertilizes the mass, drives the female from the nest, and begins guard duty. He protects the nest from predators and fans the eggs with his fins to keep them aerated and free from sediment. The eggs hatch in six to ten days depending on water temperature, and the compact school of fry remains near the nest a few days before dispersing. The male guards the fry until they leave.

Cat fans fishing during the spawn may notice a sharp drop in catch rates because male catfish take little or no food while protecting the nest. Fortunately, the spawn is over in a few days. And because fish in a system don't all spawn at the same time, a section of river or lake may contain prespawn, spawn, and postspawn catfish. If water conditions are favorable, some active feeders will always be available to catch, so there may be no noticeable decline in fishing success. If poor fishing is noticed and can't be attributed to other causes, the angler can wait a few days until the spawning peak passes and male cats are feeding once again.

Spawning Season Tactics

Two rather unusual forms of catfishing were derived to take advantage of the catfish's cavity-nesting habits. Noodling, also called hogging and grabbling, is the practice of catching catfish with one's hands when they are in nest cavities (natural and manmade) and easily cornered. In a modification of this technique called bucket fishing, participants submerse weighted buckets or drums with a semicircular hole cut in the lid. Cats enter the containers to spawn and are captured by lifting the containers from the water using an attached line. This technique is highly effective. A ten-bucket line I helped run in a Louisiana lake produced ten channel catfish daily on three days in late May.

In waters where catfish are abundant, removing a few ready-to-spawn fish from the population is no more detrimental than removing a few egg-filled bluegills. However, we should all temper our catch-and-eat desires with some common sense catch and release. Keep a few smaller cats to eat, and release larger fish. Remember: today's releases are tomorrow's trophies.

Seasonal Movements in Rivers

As the seasons change, so do the home sites of catfish.

River catfish are like ducks. They can't fly, but just like waterfowl, many catfish—blues and channel cats, in particular—migrate with the seasons. In fall, schools of cats move downstream to wintering areas, just as flocks of ducks fly south to their wintering grounds. When spring rolls around, catfish return to upstream areas to spawn, much like ducks flying north to breeding grounds.

Catfishermen who study seasonal migration habits of catfish can enjoy better fishing success throughout the seasons.

The seasonal migrations of catfish don't cover thousands of miles as is the case with our feathered friends, but their movements are significant enough—from a few miles to several hundred miles—to be worthy of our attention. Duck hunters must know where the birds are gathered in order to be successful and so, too, must catfish anglers.

Platte River Study

A study conducted in Nebraska's lower Platte River, a tributary of the Missouri River, exemplifies the movement patterns existing in many small to mid-sized rivers. Thirty-eight adult channel cats implanted with radio transmitters were tracked in this river. Their movements showed distinct seasonal trends.

During spring, 54 percent moved upstream, and 46 percent made only local movements—short movements (short movements between resting and feeding areas). During summer, 7 percent of movement was upstream, 86 percent local, and 7 percent downstream. During autumn,

Anglers often think of channel catfish as sedentary creatures, but big ones like this sometimes migrate considerable distances. Knowing where these fish go and when allows the fisherman to find his quarry throughout the seasons.

33 percent of movement was local, and 67 percent was downstream. During winter, 100 percent of movement was downstream. Catfish traveled the longest distances in spring and autumn. Spring movements averaged 11.5 river miles with a range of 1.2 to 30.1 river miles. Average autumn movement was 26.1 river miles with a range of 2.5 to 74.5 river miles.

According to the researchers, these movement patterns suggest overwintering of channel catfish in deep scour pools in the Missouri River, followed by upstream spring movements to spawning and feeding areas, and a return downstream in autumn and winter to avoid ice cover in shallow streams. The movements correspond with changing temperature and discharge patterns in the river.

Additional Evidence

A study in the lower Wisconsin and upper Mississippi Rivers (Iowa and Wisconsin) found that many channel cats (44 to 84 percent, depending on the year) migrated from the smaller Wisconsin River into the Mississippi River to overwinter. In spring, most movement was in the opposite direction from the Mississippi into the Wisconsin.

We can't say channel cats always behave the same in other waters, but the movements described above are similar to those observed in many other small to mid-sized rivers.

Movements of Blue Cats and Flatheads

Blue catfish are even more mobile than channel cats with migrations often spanning several hundred miles. Again, however, movements follow general seasonal patterns—upstream in spring and downstream in fall with more local movements during other seasons. In the Mississippi River, for example, blue cats migrate downstream to wintering areas where water is warmest. By early summer, they have returned to upstream reaches.

Numerous studies involving river flatheads show these fish are very sedentary. They

Big blue cats like this may migrate hundreds of miles each year. They typically move upstream spring to prime spawning sites and downstream in fall to wintering sites. During other seasons, movements are more restricted.

Flatheads are the least mobile of North America's big cats. Unlike blues and channel cats, which may move many miles as the seasons change, flatheads usually stay in the same areas year-round, rarely moving more than a mile from their homesite.

establish preferred use areas and seldom move far from those sites regardless of the season. To use one example, adult flatheads monitored from June through January in Mississippi's Big Black and Tallahatchie rivers moved less than one-half mile on average from their capture site during the entire six-month period.

Applying knowledge of these movements can help anglers determine where catfish are most likely to be throughout the seasons, thus increasing the chance of catching fish. Look for flatheads in the same locales season after season. Blues and channel cats concentrate near upstream spawning areas in small to mid-sized rivers in summer and near deep wintering holes in larger rivers during cold months. During spring and fall, they're on the move and may be caught almost anywhere. Adjust your tactics as necessary to pinpoint active fish.

Dog Days Cats

Learning this trio of feeding patterns will help you hook more summer catfish.

To catch catfish on a regular basis, the angler must acquire an understanding of the primary feeding patterns specific to these fish. What are catfish likely to be eating? When? Where? Armed with the answers to these questions and a considerable measure of patience and luck, the fisherman can expect to find and hook a beefy cat. Without these answers, luck alone determines the outcome.

Catfishermen must also realize that feeding patterns differ with the seasons. Different foods are available in different places during different seasons, and knowing which are available where and when is the key to finding and catching cats.

Herewith are three summer patterns you should know.

Skipjack Patterns

Skipjack herring are common in nearly all big rivers inhabited by blue cats. They comprise a major portion of the blue cat's diet in some

Anglers who understand how to pattern summer catfish find this a blue-ribbon season for hooking trophy fish.

areas, and many catfishermen use them for bait. They're easily captured in cast nets or on small jigs.

Like shad, skipjacks are active baitfish, moving about continuously in large schools. Unlike shad, however, which feed primarily on microscopic plants and animals, skipjacks are

In many waters, skipjack herring are favored foods of catfish. Find schools of these baitfish, and cats are usually nearby.

piscivorous. Minnows, shad, and other small fishes are their favored foods. This fact makes them doubly attractive to blue cats, especially in late summer. Here's why.

In July and August, large schools of skipjacks often churn the surface of the water as they pursue young-of-the-year shad. This is a highly visible phenomenon, quite similar to the surface-feeding melees of stripers and white bass. You can see the fish swirling near the surface with little shad jumping all about as they try to elude the skipjacks. This activity usually occurs near dawn and dusk, frequently near creek mouths or at the junction of two big rivers.

When surfacing skipjacks are sighted, it's highly likely scores of blue cats are lurking below. They're attracted not only by the prospect of a skipjack entrée but also by the many dead and crippled shad left behind when skipjacks slash through a school. Sometimes striped or white bass join the feeding frenzy, too, working on skipjacks and shad alike. This increases the number of injured baitfish fluttering about, another drawing card for gluttonous blues.

For the dyed-in-the-wool blue cat angler, this is a setting like no other. A 1/64- to 1/32-ounce silver or white jig cast toward swirling fish will usually garner a strike from a skipjack that can be used for bait. Cut the skippy in small pieces, run a hook through one, then cast it toward the swirls and let it fall enticingly to hungry blues waiting below. Better yet, come prepared with a few small shad ready to rig.

Following the Schools
During summer's heat, catfish in reservoirs and rivers often move to deep pools and channel edges following schools of baitfish and searching for suitable temperature and oxygen levels. Baitfish are continually seeking comfort zones where plankton, young-of-the-year

baitfish, and other foods are available. They may move several times and several miles during a twenty-four-hour period, or they may remain relatively stationary. Wherever they go, however, cats will follow with most holding in loose schools beneath the baitfish where they feed.

Find the baitfish, and you'll find the catfish; that's the key to capitalizing on this pattern. One way is using sonar to probe deep-water habitats for big fish holding beneath baitfish schools. Most will be on or near prominent bottom structure like channel breaks, humps, and holes—within the thermocline in stratified waters. When the angler sees "blips" indicating the possibility of a big cat beneath schooling baitfish at a specific depth, he anchors his craft, counts off the right amount of line, and places a piece of cutbait or a live baitfish in front of a fish. Some use a "stacked minnow" rig in this situation. Several large minnows are hooked through both lips on a single hook. These are then presented at the proper depth beneath a float. Catfish find the struggling school of crippled baitfish irresistible.

Drift-fishing with multiple poles is a good way to zero in on often-scattered schools of hot-weather catfish.

Drift-fishing is another method for finding scattered catfish in summer. Wind or a trolling motor moves the boat, while the angler watches a depth sounder and guides the craft along bottom channels and other structures where catfish are holding.

Many use a float rig for this type of fishing. The main line is run through the eye of a pencil weight, and a barrel swivel is tied below it to keep the weight from sliding down. A twelve- to eighteen-inch leader is then tied to the lower eye of the swivel. A bobber or float is affixed in the middle of the leader, and a Kahle hook is tied at the end. The float suspends the baited hook above the bottom to help prevent snags.

Drifting Bait in Small to Mid-Sized Streams

Small to mid-sized streams often serve up excellent summer catfishing. If water levels don't fall too low in the smaller streams, cats may migrate in from big lakes and rivers to take advantage of cooler water temperatures, higher oxygen levels, and plentiful food animals, such as crayfish, baitfish, and aquatic insects. The best fishing is usually at night, and most cats are caught by drifting natural bait beneath a bobber.

Bobbers can be clipped or pegged in place on the line, but this rigging is cumbersome to cast. A sliding-bobber rig works better because the bobber slides freely on the line, allowing you to reel terminal tackle close to the rod tip for easier casting. The bobber style is determined by current and bait size. In heavy current or when medium or large baits are used, use a larger, rounder, more buoyant bobber. In low or moderate flow or when small baits are used, a smaller cigar-shaped bobber is OK. The best baits are crayfish, creek minnows, or small sunfish, caught, when possible, in the water you're fishing.

Night fishing with a bobber/live-bait drift rig often produces big cats such as this when small to mid-sized rivers are targeted.

Drifting bait beneath a bobber in a cool stream is a good way to nab a mess of good-eating dog-days catfish.

Position the bobber stop so the bait hangs slightly above, not on, the stream bottom. Add enough weight to hold the bait down, then allow the rig to drift naturally, guiding it alongside catfish cover and structures. With practice and a long rod to keep your line off the water, you can become adept at steering the rig past holding areas with little worry about hang-ups.

Keep a tight line at all times. Slack line will bow downstream ahead of the bait. This leaves you in a bad position for setting the hook. Snatching slack line out of the water leaves no force in the rod's swing to drive the hook home.

Release line as the bait moves downstream. If the rig hangs up, your bobber will tip over or stop. Lift it a bit to get the bait moving again.

Then tease the rig around boulders, ease it alongside fallen trees, and work it through holes below rapids. Drift through one side of a hole, then down the other, and finally right down the middle. If nothing happens after you've worked an area thoroughly, move your bobber stop up and drift through deeper. Or move downstream to another spot and try again.

These are just a few of the many summer feeding patterns exhibited by catfish. The fishing tips offered for each scenario may or may not work in the waters you fish. If they do, hallelujah. If they don't . . . well, learn to pattern catfish yourself. What are they eating? When? Where? Those are the questions you must answer. How? Examine the stomach contents of the next catfish you catch and the next and the next. You'll find the answers there.

Turnover Time

The fall turnover period doesn't have to be the nemesis many anglers perceive it to be.

Autumn is a golden season for catfishing fans. Summer's crowds have vanished. Lakes and streams shimmer beneath canopies of vermilion and amber leaves. Summer-fattened catfish are in prime condition, offering exciting possibilities for action-hungry anglers.

This season offers some of the year's best catfish action. But it is also a time of transition. The weather changes. Air and water temperatures cool. Catfish are on the move—shallow one week, deep the next. Where fish nailed most anything yesterday, they refuse everything today. As autumn approaches, many catfish anglers cringe with frustration because their favorite fish are so hard to figure out.

You'll often hear this referred to as the "fall turnover" season because the water is "turning over" as the cooling surface layer sinks and warmer bottom water is pushed upward. Some catfish anglers write this off as a terrible time to fish. But turnover needn't be the nemesis many perceive it to be. Catfish fans can actually benefit from this fall phenomenon if they understand it.

What is fall turnover?

During summer, many lakes stratify into three distinct layers. These lakes have a layer of cold, poorly oxygenated water on the bottom and a

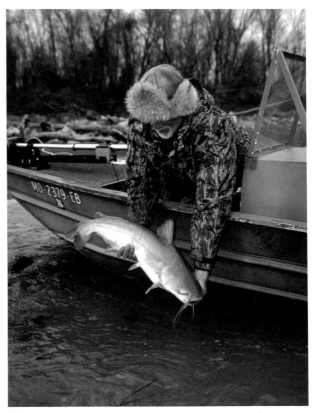

When air and water temperatures plummet in fall, catfishing may become uncomfortable for the angler, but catfish continue actively feeding and remain catchable for savvy anglers.

layer of warm, moderately oxygenated water on top. Since cold water is heavier than warm water (to a certain degree), the warmer water stays on top and colder water sinks to the bottom. In between lies a layer of cool, oxygen-rich water called the thermocline. Summer catfish usually stay in or near the thermocline in stratified lakes because that layer best satisfies their needs for proper oxygen levels and water temperature.

In late summer, fall, or early winter (the exact time depends largely on the latitude in which the lake lies), cool weather begins lowering the surface water temperature. As the upper layer cools, it becomes heavier and sinks. This action forces the warmer, lighter water below back to the surface. This water is subsequently cooled, just as the previous surface layer was, and descends as it cools. This mixing or "turnover" continues for several weeks until the thermocline

Moderate water temperatures in autumn allow river cats to reoccupy oxbows and backwaters that were too hot in the summer.

disappears and all water in the lake is roughly the same temperature. This mixing effect also replenishes the oxygen in deep water.

The end result is that fish formerly restricted to narrow bands of acceptable oxygen and temperature levels are no longer limited in their movements. Catfish that once were barred from dropping into the coolest depths because of low oxygen levels now may roam freely to much deeper water. Likewise, where once fish could not spend extended periods in extreme shallows due to high temperatures and low oxygen levels, after turnover even these areas are acceptable. Catfish now may be found in deep waters, shallow waters, or anywhere in between.

Technically, turnover continues until the surface water temperature drops below thirty-nine degrees Fahrenheit. Water is heaviest at this temperature and sinks to the bottom. Cooler water "floats" on top. This is why lakes freeze from the top down rather than from the bottom up. And this represents the annual end of the turnover process.

How do I know when a lake is "turning over"?

The time of year when turnover occurs varies by latitude. While catfishermen in cooler areas may begin turnover strategies in September, warmer regions may not have turnover until January.

On many lakes, the turnover is clearly visible. A change in water color is evident as circulating water brings up bottom debris. The water may take on a milky or brownish tint and smell like rotten eggs or decaying vegetation.

Turnover in some lakes is invisible and therefore confusing even to those familiar with the phenomenon. In these waters, the only indication turnover is occurring may be distinct changes in catfish behavior after a few weeks of cool weather. For instance, catfish caught on deep humps one week may be ambushing baitfish near shorelines the next.

Some waters don't experience turnover because they don't stratify in summer. Most rivers are a case in point. So are many large, shallow, windswept lakes and some reservoirs with lock-and-dam facilities or hydroelectric generators. In extreme Southern areas, South Florida for example, temperatures may not drop low enough for turnover to occur.

What problems are associated with turnover fishing?

The biggest problem most anglers face is pinpointing fish. In summer, most catfish could be found in or near the thermocline. Shallow-water action might have been good during cool, low-light periods, but you could be certain no cats would be caught in the "dead zone" below the thermocline.

Fall turnover drastically changes all this. With acceptable levels of oxygen from top to bottom and no discernible temperature change from the shallowest shallows to the deepest depths, catfish can be almost anywhere.

Can I overcome this problem?

Yes. The secret to turnover success is realizing that catfish still concentrate in areas that provide the most comfortable living conditions and then learning to identify those areas. Theoretically, conditions are now such that catfish can live anywhere within the lake. In actuality, factors such as oxygen content, light penetration, and food availability still greatly influence a catfish's choice of living quarters.

Consider, for instance, that all the debris and poorly oxygenated water being pushed upward from the lake bed when turnover begins temporarily "trashes" the whole system. Catfish respond by seeking areas with better water quality. To find them, anglers should do likewise. An easy way to do this is to work tributaries bringing fresh water into the lake. Another way is to look for areas where turnover has not begun. On some large lakes, different arms of the lake turnover at different times, and anglers can concentrate their efforts in areas that aren't visibly affected.

When turnover causes excessive amounts of decaying debris to circulate in the water column, sudden significant drops in the oxygen level can result. When this happens, catfish must find oxygenated water immediately. They frequently solve the problem by going directly to the nearest source, which is surface aeration from wind and waves. Consequently, windswept shorelines in fairly shallow cover may be productive catfishing spots.

Are there other good turnover hotspots?

Brushy treetops and standing timber are classic catfish cover, and they don't get any more classic than during autumn when catfish concentrate in woody areas along channel breaks. When weed beds have begun to die and decay late in the fall, cats often migrate to open lake areas where inundated trees line long underwater creek and river channels. Here the fish can move shallow or deep as water and weather conditions dictate. On cloudy or windy days when light won't penetrate very far into the water, cats may actually be found within a few feet of the surface. Bright, sunny, post-frontal days may find them hugging the bottom. Again, you'll have to experiment to find the most productive depth, keeping on the move until you locate one of the few structures holding fish. But once a cat is landed, several can often be taken with just a few well-placed casts.

The places you can find fall catfish action are almost innumerable. Long sloping points are

If the water rises to cover it, this brush-covered hump in mid-lake will be a prime hotspot for turnover catfish.

always a good possibility, as are humps and inundated islands. Cats like old fencerows that run from shallow to deep water, and large trees that have toppled into fairly deep water near the shoreline should definitely be investigated. Other favorite areas include Christmas tree fish attractors, timbered areas edging underwater ditches and ponds, submerged rock piles, stump fields, and saddle areas between two islands.

Fishing vertical structures, such as this lock-wall edge, is a good way to zero in on cats during the final weeks of fall turnover.

I've heard that catfish often hold near ledges in fall. Is this true?

During the final few weeks of turnover as the water starts to clear, catfish often concentrate on vertical structures. This is some type of bottom feature that offers great depth variance with little or no horizontal movement necessary. Good examples are bluff banks, lock-wall edges, bridge pilings, and fast-dropping slopes along creek and river channels. In such places, catfish can alter their depth according to prevailing light penetration and other factors by merely moving up or down the structures as conditions dictate.

Because catfish orienting to vertical structures can be anywhere between the bottom to mid-depths, pinpointing them may require extra effort. Begin by thoroughly fishing different depths until fish are located. If the water is still discolored, light penetration will be restricted, and catfish may move shallower. Thus, the angler may want to begin by fishing shallow reaches. As the water clears, however, bright sunlight will drive most catfish into the depths or under heavy cover. In this situation, fish first around deeper hideouts.

The key is to efficiently check a variety of depths until a catfish is caught. Then work that depth thoroughly for additional fish. When you've established the level where fish are holding, move to other vertical structures and work the same depth. Chances are good you'll encounter more catfish at some point along the way.

Are there pointers on the best time of day to fish? The best baits?

Generally, most summer anglers enjoy their best fishing during low-light periods: morning, late afternoon, or night. During autumn, however, catfish are more prone to feed all day long instead of just during morning and evening. The sun is lower in the sky, and days are shorter. Thus, conditions are good for consistent action throughout the day.

Freshly caught baitfish, such as shad, are first-rate enticements for big autumn catfish. Fish them live when targeting flatheads, or prepare them as cutbait for big blues and channel cats.

As for the best baits to use during this time of year, it's strictly a matter of what you like best. Live fish catch more flatheads. Herring and shad cutbaits are hard to beat for blue cats. Channel cats feed on their usual smorgasbord of dinner items, everything from night crawlers to commercial stinkbait, but the bigger

Rivers don't "turn over" like many lakes, so anglers can fish these flowing waters and avoid the trauma of "turnover turmoil." Trophy cats are easier to find in this season because they're more likely to be roaming the shallows.

ones are likely to fall for live fish baits or cutbaits made from fresh fish.

What about river fishing this time of year?

Because rivers are relatively unaffected by turnover, they provide an excellent alternative for anglers dealing with "turnover turmoil." In summer, high temperatures may drive river catfish to deep-water haunts, usually in or near the main river channel. Autumn offers more moderate water temperatures, allowing catfish to reinvade shallow, off-channel areas where they were found during the spring. During this season more than others, they're often found in backwaters, river-connected oxbows, and other areas where current is negligible. Because the water in these areas is shallower, these catfish are easier to find, too. And they're often more aggressive than they were during the hottest days of summer—hungry and eager to bite.

During the late weeks of summer and early weeks of fall, look for river cats near wing dikes, log jams, big snags, and other current-breaking structures in or near the main body of the river. As air and water temperature drop and autumn gets in full swing, you'll find a lot of them near

A prime site for river cats in fall, this brushy bend offers the kind of cover and structure almost sure to attract good numbers of hefty whiskerfish.

willows, cypress trees, and other woody cover off the main river in oxbows and backwaters. As autumn turns to winter, look for catfish moving back to deep-water haunts near the main river channel.

Is there anything else I should know?

Be patient and persistent. Turnover forces fish to roam, thus fishermen must also be willing to move frequently, forsaking likely looking spots or those that produced yesterday. If the tactics covered here don't produce catfish, improvise another strategy and keep trying.

The transition from summer to autumn is jolting for both fish and fishermen. Catfish find their once secure world literally turned over on them. Catfish anglers find their quarry more unpredictable than ever. Overcoming this seasonal nemesis will require all the skill, knowledge, and patience you can muster. But when you finally zero in on a big autumn cat, you're sure to agree that the rewards make the extra effort worthwhile.

Popsicle Pond Cats

When temperatures plummet, head for the nearest farm pond.

It was a polar afternoon. Alex Hinson and I were catfishing in a small farm pond.

I'd done it once before—fishing for pond catfish in the dead of winter, that is. Nearly thirty years have passed, but I remember vividly the enormous stringer of channel cats I caught that wintry day. I was twelve and hungry for some fishing, so I grabbed a rod and reel and a box of chicken livers from my grandmother's freezer. Soon, I was standing in snow on the bank of my uncle's fish pond, casting to the big cats that lurked therein but never really expecting to catch one.

To my surprise, the catfish were extraordinarily cooperative. I'd cast a bait into deep water by the dam, and before it hit bottom, a channel cat would take it. One after another, I hauled them in. I'd caught plenty of catfish before, including quite a few jumbos, but nothing like that afternoon. In less than two hours, I had twenty fat cats croaking atop the snow.

I shared the story with Alex one day, who suggested we plan another winter junket immediately. And so within the week we found ourselves sitting in a johnboat over a deep hole in the pond, dropping liver-baited hooks into the murky depths. Before each bait touched down, a sassy channel cat or bullhead would have it. Alex caught a five-pound channel cat then its twin. I caught several over three plus a two-pound yellow bullhead. Twenty-three cats fell prey to our tactics.

Active Winter Feeding

Many catfishermen still labor under the false impression that catfish don't bite in winter.

Fish a farm pond in winter? For catfish? Some might think it futile, but author Keith Sutton shows the result of a few hours fishing on a cold winter day.

That's not true. Take channel cats and bullheads, for instance. The experiences I outlined above show the exciting potential for catching these fighters during cold months. Even more amazing is the fact that both species are now common targets for ice fishermen in Northern states. Despite popular misconceptions, they don't lie in the mud and sulk when it's cold. They actively hunt food and bite readily even when lakes and rivers are frozen.

Pond Pointers

If it's eating-sized cats you're after, head straight for the nearest farm pond. Many are stocked with channel cats and/or bullheads, and despite what you may have thought, winter is the best season for catching them in these environments. You can expect good action December through February in the far North, in the deep South, and all points between. Expect the best pond catfishing, however, when the water temperature is between forty and fifty-five degrees.

Start by asking the pond owner to point out the deepest hole in the pond. During cold weather, that's where most cats will be. Fish from a boat if you can, lowering bait straight down into the hole. My typical rig consists of a 5/0 Daiichi octopus hook with a couple of split shot crimped on the line a foot above. When it reaches the bottom, I turn the reel handle a few cranks so the bait is a foot or so above the substrate where cats can better detect it. When bank fishing, I use a one-ounce Rubbercor sinker instead of split shoot and add a small cigar-shaped crappie cork on the line between the hook and sinker to float the bait just off the bottom.

Chicken liver is a top bait in this situation. Cats quickly zero in on the scent and taste of poultry blood dissolving from the tissue. Some catters prefer frozen livers because they stay on the hook better, but fresh liver has more cat-attracting qualities. Weave your hook through each piece several times, and you shouldn't have too much problem keeping it on.

Don't sit in one spot too long. If a cat is nearby, you'll have a bite before fifteen minutes passes. If you don't, move a short distance and try again. If catfish are biting, the action may end abruptly after you've caught a few fish. Once again, it's time to move and try another location.

When you're fishing for cats in winter, it pays to keep moving anyway just so you can keep warm. This is not a sport for anglers who detest the cold. You'll get chilly out there even when you're wearing the proper clothing. Your teeth will chatter, and your hands and feet will feel like popsicles.

The nice thing is when the cats start biting, that frigid feeling disappears. Nothing in the world warms you quicker than battling a rod-bending cat.

Bullheads, like channel cats, are often stocked in ponds and provide great winter action for the catfish fan.

Baits

Topwater Temptations

Catfish are bottom feeders, right? Not always, friend.

If you were to bump into one of your friends every time you visited a particular restaurant, you might start believing that's the only place your friend ever eats. That's not likely to be true, of course, but it might seem so nevertheless.

A similar situation exists between catfish and catfish anglers. Because we usually find catfish feeding on the bottom of our favorite lake, river, or pond, we have a tendency to think they always feed on bottom. This is a common misconception. In reality, catfish often feed at mid-depths, and if concentrations of nutri-

tious foods can be found in surface strata, these whiskered warriors will actually feed right on top. Just ask any fish farmer who feeds his cats commercial chow.

Two natural foods that encourage a topwater bite are grasshoppers and cicadas. I've watched catfish slurping them from the surface on many calm summer mornings, evenings, and nights. Other insects are eaten, as well: mayflies, moths, caddis larvae, and hellgrammites, for example. But these miniscule offerings don't seem to appeal to larger cats the way a big buzzing cicada or fat grasshopper does.

Grasshoppers don't rate high on the list of the most popular catfish baits, but a big juicy hopper presented tantalizingly on the surface is a great enticement for jumbo cats.

My catfishing uncle taught me another trick that never fails. Secure the hopper to a 1/0 or 2/0 gold Aberdeen crappie hook with a small rubber band, then flip it up beside a log or stump using a fly rod. You'll see every vicious strike and enjoy a rod-bending battle with each hungry cat. Catfishing was never more fun!

Cicadas

Cicadas, sometimes called locusts, spend most of their lives underground—up to seventeen years in some cases. When they emerge, they climb onto trees, shed their familiar shells, and start making the weird high-pitched noises we all associate with summer. It's tough to obtain them for bait, but on rare years when several year classes of cicadas emerge at once,

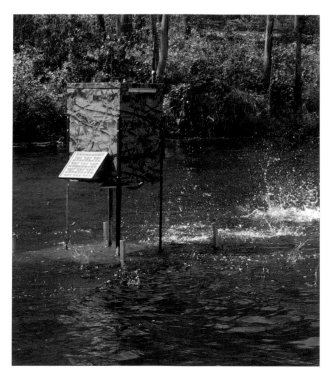

Topwater baits may seem preposterous to some anglers, but despite popular misconceptions, catfish readily take foods on the water's surface. For example, catfish churn the surface when given floating fish chow at aquaculture operations.

Grasshoppers

Because grasshoppers stay in grassy areas, not trees, they're much easier to catch than cicadas. And you don't have to wait until that special year to find an abundance. I've often pulled my boat up to a grassy margin on a river and caught several dozen. A good trick an uncle taught me is to spread an old flannel blanket across the grass and drive the hoppers to it. Their feet stick in the fabric. A fine mesh insect net, available at many pet stores, works well, too.

A friend likes to drift hoppers beneath a float on some of the Ozark streams he fishes. In my experience, they work equally on the surface, at mid-depths, or on the bottom. For real fun, though, fish them on top.

Cicadas are large insects, a fact that makes them a desirable food source for catfish, particularly in summer when these insects are abundant.

millions may cover the trees, making it much easier to find and catch them. All you need is a cricket cage to stuff them in and some youngsters who think bait catching is as much fun as fishing.

During one such year here in my native Mid-South, the buzzing of millions of cicadas filled the air with a steady hum, and the cicadas themselves filled the bellies of many catfish I caught. While fishing on a small lake, my father-in-law and I watched as dozens of cats—some of them quite large—rose to the surface to pick off cicadas that had taken a dip. A trip to the trees edging the bank provided plenty for bait. We hooked each through the hard shell on the back with a 3/0 octopus hook and cast on the water's surface with no weight, bobber, or other terminal tackle. Within seconds of each cast, we'd be playing a nice channel cat—and occasionally a blue cat—that rose to take the insect offering.

The next month, while fishing with a veteran catfisherman on Missouri's Osage River, I tried unsuccessfully to coax him into using cicadas for bait. He refused, thinking it nothing more than folly. When we pulled into the boat ramp eight hours later having caught no catfish, we were greeted by one of the man's friends who had been far more successful. "How'd you catch those?" the cat man asked, eyeballing the pile of five- to twenty-pound channels and blues in his friend's boat. "On cicadas," his friend answered. "I wasn't getting a bite on regular baits, but every time a cicada buzzed down and hit the water, a big cat would gobble it up. So I caught some and put 'em on a hook. Caught a cat on every cast. Never knew until today you could catch a cat on a topwater bait. And boy is it fun!"

Frogs for Trophy Channel Cats

Hook an amphibian to entice those giant whiskerfish.

Channel catfish aren't finicky eaters. They'll eat almost anything catfishermen offer. If you want to be consistently successful and catch lots of fish, however, be selective about the baits you use. Some are decidedly better than others.

Consider frogs, for example. If trophy channel cats are your quarry, these amphibians make hopping good lures. Small catfish relish them as well, but as a rule, the cats thus enticed are larger than average.

Master Angler Evidence

Records maintained by the Nebraska Game and Parks Commission exemplify this fact. During the ten-year period I studied, frog baits were used to catch eighty-six channel cats entered in the state's Master Angler Award program. These fish measured up to four feet long and thirty-six pounds and included many specimens in the sixteen- to twenty-seven-pound range—trophy channel cats in anybody's book. Qualifying fish were caught every month in a broad spectrum of waters—ponds, large and small reservoirs,

Check local fishing regulations for restrictions before using frogs as bait. Water-loving species work best, particularly the larger more common ones, such as bullfrogs, leopard frogs, green frogs, and pickerel frogs. Those with a body length of four to six inches are ideal.

Catching and Keeping Frogs

Sometimes you'll find them for sale in bait shops, but you also can catch frogs yourself. This is easily done by driving a rural road on a warm rainy spring night. Pick an area where traffic volume is low, and take a friend along. When the quarry is spotted, the passenger hops out, catches it, and places it in a lidded minnow bucket to which a little water has been added. Walking rain-dampened roads with a flashlight and a dampened pillow case for frog storage is also effective. It's possible to gather dozens of frogs this way on a single night.

Frogs are among the most overlooked yet most effective live baits for jumbo channel cats.

large and small rivers, irrigation canals, and more—indicating the versatility of frog baits under widely varying conditions.

You also can catch frogs by hand or with a small-mesh dip net along the shores of ponds, lakes, backwaters, bayous, and streams; in adjacent grass and weeds; or along the water's edge at night by shining a blinding light at them.

The leopard or grass frog, a common species throughout much of the United States, is among several species of aquatic frogs commonly used for catfish bait.

Live frog-bait rigs are simple—just a hook on the line and maybe a couple of split shot to carry the bait down. Hook the frog through a foreleg to keep it lively.

Store frogs in a cool place inside a dampened container to keep them lively.

Frog Rigs and Tactics

Most users hook frogs through both lips or in the thigh. I've learned, however, that hooking the amphibian through a foreleg maintains maximum swimming ability, making the frog a more enticing bait. I prefer using a 5/0 to 6/0 weedless hook that has a wire guard to prevent snagging in weeds or brush. In lieu of this, I use a similarly sized octopus or Kahle hook. Adding a couple of split shot on the line twelve inches above the hook completes the rig. No bobber is necessary.

This rig can be fished several ways. I like using a sturdy twelve- to sixteen-foot fiberglass or graphite crappie jigging pole to work the bait in beds of lily pads in ponds or shallow lakes. Position yourself along the pads, and reach out with the pole to ease the frog into small openings. Slack off to let it swim. You also can place the frog on a pad and let it jump off. Be ready, however, for the ensuing explosion. Lily pads are favored haunts for giant channel cats, and despite misconceptions, these fish will hit frogs on top, providing unparalleled thrills.

An equally effective tactic is casting the frog near catfish cover using a spinning or bait-casting outfit. The frog will immediately swim for the bottom, where it's easily spotted by foraging cats. If a bite is not forthcoming within a few minutes, raise your rod tip to stir the frog into action again. Most strikes come quickly when the bait is swimming. Lack of action should prompt you to relocate to another fishing area.

Strangely, few catfishermen use frog baits. I suggest you follow the Cornhuskers' lead. Live frogs will catch trophy channel cats no matter where you fish.

Mussel-Bound Blues

When mussels are on the menu, blue cats gather around the feeding trough.

If you've never used mussel meat for blue cat bait, you ought to give it try. Next to baitfish, freshwater mussels or "clams" are among the blue cat's favorite foods in waters where they are available. In fact, some ardent anglers claim blue cats like mussels better than baitfish. Channel and flathead cats eat them, too, but not with the same gusto of their larger relatives.

The Facts According to Joe Mathers

Joe C.K. Mathers was one of the first to write about the efficacy of mussels in his 1953 booklet *Catfishin'*. He rated them "excellent to superior" as cat bait and described how to use them.

"Remove from shells and use fresh or still better allow to sour for a day or two in an open container with plenty of 'clam juice' covering them,"

Catfish feed on many species of mussels from the tiny Asiatic clam to the mid-sized deertoe and even the very large yellow sandshell.

he wrote. "Steam over a fire to toughen before souring if you want a tougher bait. If soured 'just right' (sour, not rotten, determine by smelling), clams are one of the best catfish baits especially during mid-summer when few other baits are giving results. They make a tough, luring bait usable on all kinds of lines. Freshwater clams are found in ponds, lakes, and streams, certain kinds of flowing waters, and others in quiet waters. Collect in shoreline shallows or gather by dragging bottom areas with clamming hooks. Or, if there is a clamming industry along your river, just get a bucket of flesh after they have steamed off the shells."

The "clamming industry" Mathers refers to began in the late 1800s and continued through the early 1950s. During that period, most buttons on clothing were made from mussel shells. In fact, mussel harvesting and the button-making industry were big business throughout the Mississippi River Valley. Many river families made a living collecting mussels from the bottoms of our big rivers. Some dived to collect these mollusks. Others used clamming hooks, also known as crow's-foot dredges or brails. Each consisted of a long wooden or metal bar from which dangled numerous blunt four-pronged hooks attached with short lines. The entire unit was lowered into a river and slowly pulled downstream. The hooks raked the bottom and touched open mussels, which promptly closed on the hooks. Captured mussels were then hauled to the surface and removed from the brail.

Once collected, the mussels were "cooked out" along the river banks. Mussels were dumped in cauldrons of hot water so the fleshy insides could be easily separated from the valuable outer shell. The shells were then shipped to factories for processing into buttons.

The mussel-shell button industry died after the advent of plastics during World War II. But freshwater mussel shells are still important moneymakers for some people. Today, mussel shells are used primarily in the cultured pearl industry centered in Japan. The shells (usually collected by divers using scuba gear) are shipped overseas and processed into pearl nuclei by stripping the outer layer and punching appropriate-sized blanks into round pellets. These round mother-of-pearl nuclei are then inserted into pearl oysters suspended in cages in a suitable estuary or ocean bay.

The actual nucleus insertion procedure is a closely guarded secret of the Japanese cultured pearl industry. Oysters are allowed to secrete their own mother-of-pearl around the nucleus for six months to three years depending on the quality of pearl desired. Pearls are then harvested, graded, and sold for jewelry.

Luther's Lessons

Luther Gaither, a sheller on the White River at DeValls Bluff, Arkansas, was one of the first to pique my interest in using mussels for blue cat bait. I spent a day with him on the river, watching him go down for shells in a 175-pound diving helmet constructed from an old bomb you can do makes it suitable for eating. A lot of it we give away for hog feed. But we always keep some for blue cat bait. I'll show you what we do to it."

Gaither took me aside and showed me several plastic five-gallon buckets full of mussel meat stewing in the hot sun.

"This is the best blue cat bait ever was made," he said, smiling. "You just toss the pieces in a bucket with some juice from the steaming process and let it sit a week or so till it sours a bit. We use it on trotlines mostly and catch everything from little eatin' size cats up to the big guys weighing seventy-five pounds and more. It's extremely tough, so it stays on the hooks well. And the blue cats swarm to it like kids to a candy shop. Some of the blues we catch, if you open their stomachs, you find they're stuffed with mussels of every sort. This is their favorite food year-round, so nothing works better for bait."

My own experiments over the next several years proved Gaither right. Mussel flesh took blue cats even when they turned their noses up at fresh shad and suckers. Mostly I used it on trotlines, but I also found it an excellent rod-and-reel bait, fresh or sour. I became a convert and often stopped at one of the local shellers' riverside shanties to bum enough mussel meat for a weekend's fishing.

Unfortunately, shellers like Luther Gaither have largely disappeared. River dredging, pollution, and commercial shelling have taken a toll on the mussels, and few commercially valuable shell beds remain in most of our rivers. Fewer still are the number of people willing to collect and prepare them for market. Nevertheless, if you look hard enough, you'll probably find a sheller here and there on most of the larger rivers in the Mississippi drainage. And if you're lucky, you can drum up an acquaintance with

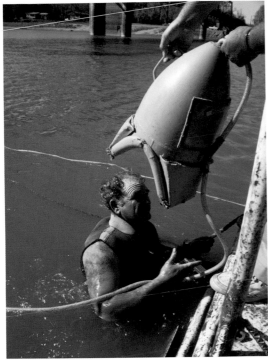

Luther Gaither prepares to dive for mussels in Arkansas's White River. His diving helmet is constructed from an old bomb casing.

casing. Air was supplied by a topside compressor, and a two-way radio allowed communication with his partner on the boat.

Later that day, Gaither showed me freshwater pearls collected from White River mussels, a collection of crow's-foot dredges, and a tubular tumbler used to sort shells by size and species. I also examined large metal vats, some fashioned from car hoods, where the mussels were steamed. When the shells opened, they were allowed to cool, and the meat was removed by hand and examined for pearls. I asked Gaither if the flesh of the mussels had any use.

"The meat's edible," he said, "but it's tough and rubbery as the soles of your boots. I guess we've tried every way in the world to fix it for eating—even grinding it up and trying to turn it into chowder meat or sausage. But nothing them and have a ready supply of mussel meat for your own blue cat forays.

Joe Drose on Mussels

In 1997, I met another blue cat angler familiar with the use of mussels for bait. Joe Drose of Cross, South Carolina, is one of the premier catfishing guides in the United States. He's been guiding full-time on lakes Marion and Moultrie—the Santee-Cooper lakes—for decades. Putting clients on giant catfish is his specialty.

"Personally, I think blue cats prefer mussels over anything they can eat," Drose told me on a February fishing trip. "In winter, most of the big cats here, the blues especially, are feeding on mussels. They move to sand edges in shallow water and stuff themselves in beds of

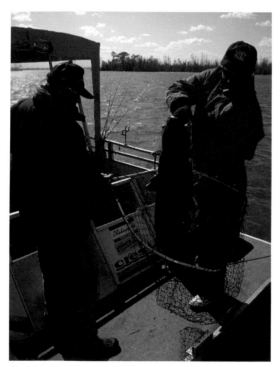

Guide Joe Drose helps a client land a nice Santee-Cooper blue cat caught while fishing one of the lakes' mussel beds.

small mussels. When the water in the lake is down, I watch for beds of shells and then come back and fish those areas because that's where the biggest fish—and the most fish—are likely to be. They'll eat on mussels in the shallows throughout the winter and up into May."

When you think about it, Drose noted, it's easy to understand why cold-water catfish feed so heavily on mussels. First of all, mussels are slow. In fact, in winter, they don't move at all. That means they're easy to catch and eat. Second, mussels live in dense colonies called beds. There are lots of them piled together in very small areas. When the water is cold, catfish congregate around these beds where they can gorge day after day with little expenditure of energy.

These same factors make mussels an excellent food source regardless of the season.

"Catfish also feed on mussels in summer," said Drose. "In late June and July, the shallow water gets real warm, and a lot of the mussels die. Many float to the top and are carried around by the current in the lakes. Catfishing folks take a dip net and dip them right up. Then they open them up, get the meat out, and fish with it. That works extremely well on our catfish."

In his book *Masters' Secrets of Catfishing*, John Phillips describes a similar phenomenon on the Tennessee River in Tennessee and Alabama. "Every year, the Asiatic clams . . . experience a die-off," Phillips writes. "The dead clams open their shells, and the little animals inside float to the surface. When the clams start dying off, catfish in the area hear the dinner bell ringing and feed on these mollusks voraciously. Oftentimes, by observing the surface of the water, you can spot dead clams lying on top, scoop the clams up, bait them on your hooks, send them right back to the bottom, and catch cats . . . Many of today's topnotch catfishermen will

Zebra mussels, an exotic species, rarely grow larger than a man's fingernail, but catfish, particularly blue cats, gorge on them wherever they are present.

When water levels are low, it pays to scout for the location of mussel beds. Return when the water rises again, and you're likely to find catfish gorging on the bounty.

locate mussel beds on major waterways, swim down, collect the mussels in states where allowed, open the shells, and bait up for catfish."

The inch-long exotic Asiatic clam (*Corbicula*), now common in many North American lakes and rivers, is a special favorite for catfish, but native mussels, especially smaller varieties like lilliputs, wartybacks, and deertoes, are also relished. The bellies of some smaller cats I've examined were full of tiny zebra mussels, the noxious invader that has colonized many United States waters. Large cats sometimes contain yellow sandshells or other mussels that may be six to eight inches long and as big around as a man's wrist.

Shell and all is eaten regardless of the mussel species. Digestive juices kill the mussel, the shell opens, the flesh inside is digested, then the shell is passed by the fish.

To find mussel beds, search near shore in three to six feet of water. They can be pinpointed by sight during low-water periods, as Drose does, or you can find them by moving parallel to shore and probing the bottom with a cane pole. The shells produce a distinctive crunching sound when the pole hits them.

Catfish return to the same beds season after season, so once a bed is found, memorize its location or mark it on a map.

Joe Drose's techniques for fishing mussel beds are easily duplicated by any angler seeking trophy-class blues. He usually anchors his boat and still-fishes using sturdy tackle: 7-foot Shakespeare Ugly Stick Tiger Rods and Shakespeare bait-casting reels spooled with twenty-five- to eighty-pound-test monofilament line.

His primary fishing rig consists of an egg sinker on the main line above a barrel swivel with an eight- to twelve-inch leader connecting the swivel to a sturdy 3/0 to 5/0 Kahle hook. This bottom-fishing rig is baited, cast to a likely spot, and allowed to sit for up to fifteen minutes. If no bite is forthcoming, Drose moves to another spot and tries again. Several rigs may be presented at each location, and they may not be baited with mussels.

"I sometimes use commercial chunk baits or pieces of hot dogs for bait," Drose tells me. "These are about the same size as the small mussels the catfish are feeding on, and they seem to work real well.

When catfish are feeding in mussel beds, they readily take other baits, as well, such as blueback herring.

feeding on mussels primarily, they won't pass up a piece of herring that's properly presented."

If you use the actual mussels for bait, remove the flesh from the shell and use it fresh. Or better still, follow Joe Mathers' and Lester Gaither's advice: allow the meat to sour for a day or two in an open container with plenty of "clam juice" covering it. If there's a shelling industry along your river, visit a local sheller to get a bucket of flesh after he's steamed off the shells. Or gather your own mussels using a dip net or by feeling for them in mud or sand bottom in shoreline shallows.

Mussels and blue cats go together like minnows and crappie. So try shellfish for catfish this season. If trophy-class blues are what you're after, mussels can make it happen.

"Most of the time we use small herring for bait," he continued. "Although the catfish are

Endangered Species or Catfish Bait?

It's easy to find and collect mussels in shallow waters of many lakes and streams, but be careful you don't collect protected species.

Be cautious when collecting mussels for catfish bait. Many species, such as the Curtis pearlymussel, turgid blossom, pink mucket, speckled pocketbook, and fat pocketbook, are protected under the Endangered Species Act. You're not likely to find these species when looking for catfish bait simply because they are rare. But fines can be stiff for disturbing or harming these endangered animals. Check with your state wildlife agency to determine what's legal where you fish.

Catching Cats on Artificial Lures

You can catch catfish on a variety of artificial lures but only if you understand what makes these lures enticing.

C an catfish be caught using artificial lures? Yes, indeed.

Consider this evidence. In 2002, anglers submitted 415 qualifying cat- fish in Nebraska's Master Angler Program, in- cluding 309 channel cats, ninety-six flatheads, and ten blue cats. No qualifying blue cats were caught on artificial lures, but twenty-two of the channel cats were (7 percent) and a whopping twenty-six of ninety-six flatheads (27 percent).

Many types of lures enticed these Nebraska cats. Crankbaits produced the most channel catfish (seven), followed by spinners/spinner- baits (five), jigs (four), plastic worms/lizards (three each), spoons (two), and topwater plugs (one). Flathead cats fell for crankbaits (ten), jigs (nine), spoons (five), and spinners (two).

Catfishermen rarely use artificial lures to entice their quarry, but if water conditions are right and the proper lure is used, cats will find the bait and strike.

Catfish use many senses to help pinpoint foods. For example, they have excellent eyesight that they use to see prey items in clear waters. When a fishing lure is seen, it, too, may be eaten.

Jigs tipped with minnows or night crawlers accounted for six of nine catches in the jig category.

How many of these cats were taken intentionally using artificials? I don't know. Program records don't include such information. I'd bet my next paycheck, however, it was few or none. Catfish fans rarely pursue their quarry with artificial lures. Most whiskerfish thus caught were probably incidental catches. While fishing for bass, walleyes, or other species, the angler nailed a dandy cat and submitted it for recognition.

Nevertheless, this information is intriguing enough to beg the question: is it possible to target catfish specifically with artificial lures? The answer is yes. If you use the right lures under the right conditions, it is likely you'll catch some catfish. Blue cats, flatheads, and channel cats all can be taken in this manner. Nebraska is at the edge of blue cat range, which accounts for the few entries in their Master Angler Program.

Understanding Catfish Senses

To increase your success using lures, it helps to understand factors influencing a catfish's food selection. To do this, we must first understand some basic facts about catfish senses.

Fact #1. Despite having tiny eyes, catfish have excellent sight. In muddy waters, good eyesight offers few benefits. But in clearer water, catfish use their acute vision to help pinpoint prey.

Fact #2. Catfish have good hearing, as well. The specialized construction of a catfish's internal auditory system allows it to detect sounds in a wide range of frequencies.

Fact #3. Low-frequency sounds undetectable to the catfish's inner ear are picked up by the lateral line. The catfish uses this system to pinpoint low-frequency vibrations emitted by food animals scurrying across the bottom, flopping at the surface, or swimming through the water.

Fact #4. The catfish's senses of taste and smell are unexcelled in the animal kingdom. The skin, whiskers, and surfaces of the mouth and gill rakers are covered with taste buds, and a highly evolved olfactory system allows catfish to smell some compounds at concentrations as minute as one part per ten billion parts of water.

Fact #5. A catfish uses as many senses as possible when searching for dinner. The sensory organs detect chemicals, sounds, vibrations, and visual stimuli from potential food items and send messages to the fish's brain telling it to find, chase, and eat the food.

What does this mean for a catfish angler fishing artificial lures? In a nutshell, it works like this. A lure that stimulates one of the catfish's senses may be attacked. A lure that stimulates two or more senses almost certainly will be attacked.

Let's say you're fishing a jig with a soft-plastic, shad body. This lure emits no sounds or scents. If you fish it in muddy water, it can't be seen, either, so it's useless as a catfish bait.

Let's say you fish that same jig in clear water. Now a catfish might take it because the lure can be seen. If you continued fishing the jig in muddy water and added a night crawler or minnow to the hook, again there's a chance of catching a cat because the fish can detect the scent or taste of the live bait added to the lure.

Now let's try a jig/minnow combo in clear water and change to a rattling jig head. Chances of catching a cat grow exponentially because now we're stimulating all the senses. Catfish can see the lure, hear it, and feel the vibrations. They can taste and smell the added live bait. Starting to get the picture?

The Right Lures in the Right Places

The best lures resemble the catfish's natural prey items, such as baitfish, crayfish, frogs, or worms. And those that resemble injured or slow-moving prey items are probably best of all, a fact to consider when making your retrieve or working your lure.

It's also important to place the lure in the specific areas within a river or lake where catfish lurk, such as channel edges, riprap, and stream bends. Remember the high percentage of Nebraska flatheads caught on lures? I'm guessing most of those lures were used by bass anglers fishing near dense woody cover. Flatheads love this type of cover, and they're quick to attack live baitfish or lures resembling live baitfish, such as many crankbaits, jigs, spoons, and spinners. If those lures were tipped with live bait (as many were) or had rattles or components that vibrated or flashed (as many did), their effectiveness was further enhanced.

So, should you target cats with artificial lures? That depends. If you prefer catching as many cats as possible, especially trophy cats, you'll probably do better sticking to "regular" cat baits. But if you enjoy more challenging en-

Why use lures when baits work better? For some catfishermen, it simply provides a welcome change of pace. And at times, using lures can be a highly effective method for catching cats.

deavors, give lures a try. Catching cats on artificials adds another fun dimension to this multifaceted sport.

Home Brews for Catfish

Catfisherman are the alchemists of angling, hoping to turn unusual concoctions of smelly ingredients into golden formulas catfish can't resist.

Catfish love stinkbait, and almost every hardcore catfish angler has a top-secret stinkbait formula whiskerfish just can't resist.

One old-timer told me, "There are more stinkbait recipes than there are food recipes, and not all of them have been invented yet. The fun part is experimenting. When you come up with a brand-new formula, you're just as proud as you'd be if you made a delicious new barbecue sauce or a tasty marinade."

After I swore on a Bible I wouldn't reveal the ingredients, this aficionado allowed me to watch as he mixed up a batch of his secret-formula cat catcher. You'd have thought he was

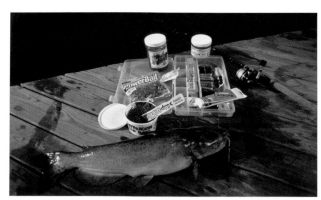

Many types of stinkbaits are available, along with a variety of paraphenalia made for fishing these specialty cat baits.

Emeril Lagasse preparing a sumptuous bisque. He whisked together a cup of this, a dollop of that and a spoonful of some top-secret ingredient. Then like a bon vivant sampling the bouquet of an expensive wine, he lifted a cupful to his nose and inhaled. Tears streamed down his reddened cheeks, his knees quaked, and it appeared he might throw up.

"Holy Moses!" he proclaimed, quivering like a headless chicken. "One whiff of that would kill a skunk. But it needs to be stronger."

Indeed, stinkbait chefs believe the worse it smells, the more catfish it will catch. To make it so, they add some rank ingredients to their brews.

Decomposing fish, for example. Heads and guts allowed to ferment several days reek like a week-old sardine sandwich, and nothing makes a catfish lick its whiskers quicker.

Limburger cheese, too. Normal humans can't eat it without holding their nose. Stinkbait manufacturers and catfish love it.

When making a batch of his locally famous Putrid Pudding—that's what he calls his rotten-fish stinkbait—one of my catfishing companions hides the container on top of his neighbor's barn. This serves three primary purposes:

1. It keeps the raccoons and neighborhood cats from getting into the bait (and possibly dying as a result);

2. It allows the brew to ferment properly in the hot sun.

3. It helps my chum avoid unnecessary exposure to the stinkbait's toxic fumes. The poor barn owner has searched unsuccessfully for years trying to pinpoint the source of the horrific stench.

To make Putrid Pudding, my friend puts two quarts of dead shad in a plastic bucket and allows them to decompose until only an oily residue remains. Then on a camp stove outside, he boils the residue and stirs in one quart of soured milk, two packets of dry yeast, and a half-pound of Limburger cheese. He heats this while adding flour and stirring until thick. The mixture then is carefully funneled into a plastic jug he plugs with cheesecloth. The jug sits on the neighbor's barn for a week or two at least, bubbling like a witch's cauldron. When my friend can detect the ghastly smell from home, he knows the stinkbait has properly aged and is ready to use.

Should the user get a drop of Putrid Pudding on his clothes, the garments must be burned. If it got on your skin, God knows what would happen. Great care must be taken to avoid contact.

My buddy handles the mix like it's radioactive waste. He fishes it by pushing a hooked square of sponge into the goo with a long stick. The sponge absorbs the mess and stays on the hook when cast.

Does he catch catfish with it? Yes, indeed. And when he goes catfishing, he has his favorite bank-fishing spot all to himself. No one can stand to fish near him.

How Stinkbaits Work

Despite popular misconceptions, stinkbaits don't work because they stink. I learned this while interviewing Dr. John Caprio of Louisiana State University, a neurophysiologist who has studied what fish taste and smell since 1971. His research has given him extraordinary insights into catfish feeding behavior.

"Catfish are swimming tongues," Caprio told me. "You can't touch any place on a catfish without touching thousands of taste buds. A six-inch catfish has more than 250,000—on the outside of its body, inside the mouth, and on the gill rakers. To use an analogy, it's as if the tip of your tongue grew out and covered your body. Consequently, the sense of taste is very keen.

"The sense of smell is equally keen," he continued. "Catfish can smell and taste some compounds at one part to ten billion parts of water. Catfish also use their lateral line to help sense

Thousands of taste buds cover the skin of a catfish with the largest concentrations of these sensory organs on the whiskers, mouth, and gill rakers. Catfish also have an extraordinary sense of smell, pumping water in and out of the paired nostrils so chemicals in the water can be detected.

prey, they can sense electrical charges in living cells, and they have an excellent sense of touch. Channel catfish have excellent sight. All these senses combined help catfish locate food."

Despite their extraordinary sensory abilities, however, catfish can't detect the odor of stinkbait that assaults a catfisherman's nose.

"What stinks to you and me doesn't stink to catfish," said Caprio. "People smell chemicals volatilized to the air, but animals living in water couldn't care less about volatiles because they can't detect them. They detect chemical compounds in the water. What you and I smell, fish can't smell."

So why do stinkbaits work? Water-soluble components of the stinkbait contact the taste buds covering a catfish's body, and when the taste buds detect these chemicals, they send a message to the fish's brain telling it to find the food. The catfish then approaches the food and picks it up. Taste buds in the mouth relay messages to another part of the brain and tell the fish to eat the food—or spit it out. In the case of good stinkbaits, they eat and consequently are caught.

Species Specifics

Small channel cats and blue cats under ten pounds are most likely to be caught by anglers fishing stinkbaits. Young fish of these species scavenge more and eat a wider variety of foods than heavyweight adults. As channel and blue cats grow in size, their diet becomes less varied, consisting mostly of live baitfish, crayfish, and other abundant forage animals. Flatheads rarely scavenge, so stinkbaits rarely catch them.

Types of Stinkbaits and Ways to Fish Them

There are several types of stinkbaits, each with a particular consistency that requires a particular method of fishing.

Dip baits, like my friend's Putrid Pudding, have the consistency of . . . well, dip—the kind you

Stinkbait anglers often include unusual ingredients in their home brews.

A pond fishermen prepares to fish a catfish worm covered with dip bait.

dunk potato chips in. (Be careful not to mistake one for the other!) They sometimes are called sponge baits because a sponged-covered treble hook is used to soak up the bait for fishing. Dip the sponge hook in the bait, squish it with a stick until it's saturated, then cast the weighted sponge rig to a spot that looks catfishy and wait for Mr. Whiskers to hone in on the scent.

Secret Recipes Revealed

Secret recipes for proven stinkbaits often are passed down from generation to generation with explicit instructions never to reveal the ingredients. I've discovered, however, that a little hooch shared by a campfire has a magical way of loosening tongues. Some recipes thus collected:

Blood & Oil Sponge Bait
Pour blood from a carton of fresh chicken livers into a jar or plastic container. Add the oil from a can of sardines or tuna. Stir. Sponge. Fish.

Knock-Out Cheese Bait
Combine equal measures of pork or beef brains or chicken liver and Limburger cheese in a plastic butter tub, mash together, cover, poke a few holes in the lid, then place in a hotspot—on the roof of your neighbor's barn, perhaps—for several days. Use as a dip bait.

Got-A-Bite Stinkbait
Mix two cups cottonseed meal, which can be purchased at farm supply stores, with two cups flour, then stir in one can condensed cheddar cheese soup, two tablespoons pancake syrup, and two tablespoons vegetable oil. Place in a zip-seal bag and refrigerate until ready to fish.

Mr. Whiskers Dough Balls
Mix in a large plastic tub one cup yellow cornmeal, one cup flour, one-quarter teaspoon anise oil, and one tin sardines packed in oil. Add small amounts of water to form a bread-like dough. Form dough into pieces the size of a ping-pong ball and drop into boiling water for three minutes. Remove, drain on paper towels, and allow to cool. Catch a cat with them.

Breakfast of Champions
Run a pint of chicken livers through a blender until liquefied. Slowly add Wheaties cereal, and continue blending until the mixture turns into a ball. Roll into golf ball size pieces and place in a zip-seal bag. Cool to firm before using.

Catfish Biscuits
Empty one can of tuna or mackerel into a mixing bowl, juice and all. Add the dough from two cans of biscuits. Mix by hand until biscuit dough and fish are well blended. Add some flour if needed to get the right consistency. Store in zip-seal plastic freezer bags. To use, pinch off a suitably sized chunk and place on a No. 4 treble hook.

Hot dogs marinated in strawberry Kool-Aid and garlic make great chunk baits.

Dip baits also can be fished on a "catfish worm," a ringed, soft-plastic lure that is dunked and covered in the smelly concoction. Dip baits melt quickly, so reapply frequently to keep it covered.

Doughbaits have pizza-dough consistency. Many won't stay hooked when casting, especially during hot weather. Cloth doughbait bags and spring-wound bait-holder treble hooks are helpful, but it's best to stick with thick dough-bait mixtures that can be molded around a reg-ular hook to form a firm ball that won't fly off when casting.

Make your own doughbait by mixing flour and water to form thick dough. Add a flavoring of your choosing—anise oil, blood, and rancid cheese are favorites—then roll the dough into balls and store in a plastic butter tub or similar container. Cool in an ice chest before fishing to firm it up.

To properly fish doughbaits, move the bait very little. Give careful thought to finding prime cat-fishing areas, then after you cast, allow the bait to sit a half hour or so. Doughbaits must melt to lay a scent trail. If there are no bites in the specified time, relocate.

Chunk baits are solid grape-sized baits. They melt slowly, so a cat must be close to find your offering unless you have time to wait. This fact, however, makes chunk baits highly desirable for baiting trotlines, limblines, and other set lines.

Make your own chunk baits by slicing inexpen-sive hot dogs into one-inch pieces and putting them in a plastic tub. Add a package of unsweet-ened strawberry Kool-Aid and two tablespoons minced garlic. Fill the tub with water, and allow the wieners to marinate overnight. Hook. Cast. Fish. Catch.

As you can imagine, creating and fishing with stinkbaits is a smelly situation. To be a true catfisherman, though, you must give it a whirl sooner or later. It's one sure route to catfishing success.

Stinkbait Precautions—Read Carefully!

A word of warning is in order here. You will notice I recommend the use of plastic containers when mixing and storing stinkbaits. This is because some stinkbait concoctions give off fermentation bubbles and gases that can cause a tightly sealed glass or metal container to explode with dangerous and gut-wrenching results. Always follow these rules when preparing stinkbaits:

- Use plastic containers, never glass or metal, for brewing and storing.

- Never tighten a lid on the mixture.

- Store all stinkbait mixtures outside at all times, preferably somewhere out of reach of animals.

Wild and Wacky Cat Catchers

Fish with whiskers eat stuff you couldn't imagine.

Catfish eat weird foods, no doubt. An 1847 edition of *Scientific American* reports, "A catfish was purchased in the Cincinnati market, lately, which, on being opened, was found to contain in its stomach a silver thimble, a gold ring, and a counterfeit dime, tied up in a rag."

The Manitoba Morning Free Press in Winnipeg (May 18, 1894) tells of a 140-pound Kansas catfish caught by one Douglass Smith. "In its stomach was found a small bottle, securely corked, containing this message: 'Whoever will find this will please send it back to me. H.E. Pipes.' Mr. Pipes had thrown the bottle in the Kaw River three years earlier, seventy-five miles from where the fish was caught."

Another weird tale of the catfish's gustatory habits comes to us via an 1867 edition of *Harper's Weekly*, which contained a story about soldiers rowing across a river who encountered a large fish floundering on the surface. "It proved to be a large cat-fish, which had swallowed a musk-rat. The animal's tail still hung out of its mouth."

In historical literature, we also find references to many unusual catfish baits. In *The Adventures of Huckleberry Finn*, for example, Huck and Jim "… bait one of the big hooks with a skinned rabbit and set it and catch a catfish that was as big as a man …" Author Mark Twain may have seen such bait being used while plying the Mississippi as a steamboat pilot.

Another literary giant, Henry Thoreau, also wrote about the catfish's indiscriminate feeding habits. Bullheads, he noted, "… will take any kind of bait, from an angleworm to a piece of tomato can, without hesitation or coquetry."

Soap

While using a tomato can as bait might be stretching your luck, there are many old-fashioned baits seldom used by today's anglers that still work wonders for enticing catfish. One such allurement is Ivory soap. Proctor & Gamble probably didn't think their product would become a popular catfish bait when it was in-

The variety of baits that can be used to catch catfish is simply astounding.

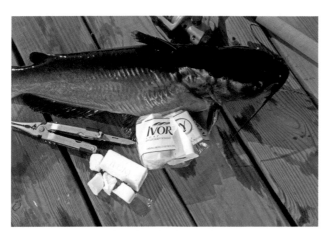

Some folks find it hard to believe, but soaps, such as Ivory, make superb catfish baits.

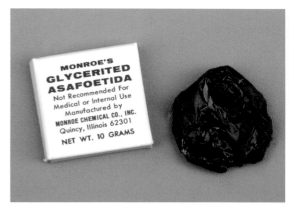

In decades past, catters often used asafetida as a cat attractant.

troduced in 1879. But it did. Hardcore catters have used it for decades with great success.

Old-timers on the rivers I fished as a youngster often baited trotlines with chunks cut from bars of Ivory soap. My uncle was one of these old-timers, and when we ran lines he'd baited in this fashion, it wasn't unusual to find a cat on every other hook. A small piece threaded on a hook works equally well for rod and reel anglers.

Although Ivory is the brand most often used, I've heard that Octagon and Zote soaps also work great. These are "pure" soaps without added scents or chemicals. Some catfishermen I know use old-fashioned lye soap made at home.

Asafetida and Other Scent Baits

Asafetida is another superb catfish enticement now largely forgotten. Also called stinking gum and Devil's dung, this product, made from plants native to Eurasia, comes in two primary forms—a resin and an oil—both of which are used to flavor foods and for medicinal purposes. In decades past, children often wore a pouch of asafetida around the neck to ward off winter

colds—an embarrassing matter for the kids, for asafetida has a strong, repugnant smell.

Catfishermen used asafetida by mixing a bit of resin or oil in a bucket of water. A cotton trotline was then soaked in the mixture. When the line was set, catfish would come and rub against it, much like a feline playing with catnip. Many got foul-hooked, thus producing a catch without the angler having to obtain regular bait. Oil of rhodium, anise oil, and rotten eggs sometimes were used the same way.

Back in the 1960s, many men with whom I catfished carried a bottle of asafetida oil in their tackle box. We'd put a few drops in a can of water then soak a piece of cloth in the mixture and put it on our hook. We caught many catfish using this scent bait, all of which ate the bait just like they might eat a worm. You probably won't find asafetida in the local drugstore like we did back then, but it's available through several Internet sources.

Something Fruity

A few anglers still use another unusual catfish bait: fruit. The idea of a catfish eating fruit stretches the imagination, but cats are opportunistic feeders that will gorge on various types of wild fruits when available. In South America, for example, the red-tailed catfish is considered especially delicious during high-water periods when it migrates into flooded jungles to feed on fruits falling into the water. Our own blue cats and channel cats are known to do likewise, gathering to feed on muscadines, mulberries, haw fruits, and even acorns and hickory nuts that drop from trees overhanging the water. When we fished flooded woodlands along the lower Mississippi when I was younger, the catfish we cleaned often had fruits and nuts in their bellies.

My father-in-law, Hansel Hill of Alpine, Arkansas, said anglers on Arkansas's Lake Greeson frequently use ripe persimmons for bait. "In fall when persimmons get ripe and start falling, it's not unusual to clean a catfish that has a belly full of them," he said. "Years ago, when folks discovered this, they started using persimmons for bait. And they learned real quick, when persimmons are available, they're one of the best catfish baits there is. I've seen folks load a boat with cats by baiting their hooks with nothing but persimmons."

On the Little Missouri River, a tributary of Lake Greeson, I've run into catfishermen using mulberries for bait. Unlike persimmons, which ripen in autumn, mulberries ripen in spring.

Persimmons are among many fruits catfish eat.

The banks along the Little Missouri have hundreds of mulberry trees overhanging the water, and when the ripe fruit starts falling, you can see schools of channel catfish fighting to grab each morsel that splashes down. The mulberry anglers gather the fruits and impale two or three on a baitholder hook. The fruit is lobbed out under a mulberry tree and rarely reaches bottom before a cat gobbles it up.

In his book *Masters' Secrets of Catfishing*, Alabama writer John Phillips reports on another top-notch fruit bait. "Golden raisins are good catfish bait if you're using set hooks, trotlines, or any method of fishing that allows the bait to be in the water for an extended time," he says. "The raisins are the most productive during the hot summer months—particularly when fishing at night … The raisins swell up on the hooks and begin to ferment, giving off a very strong odor that calls catfish. Because of the raisins' bright-yellow color, the cats can find and eat them easily."

Catfish guide Phil King of Corinth, Mississippi, often uses raisins for bait. He reports that white grapes are another fruit anglers should try. "They're a good summer bait," he says.

Bullheads and Other Catfish

Bullhead catfish are the main prey of flatheads in many waters where both are common. They've been used as bait by flathead fans since at least the nineteenth century, but nowadays, relatively few anglers ever try them despite the fact that they may be the best bait available when you're targeting trophy-class flatheads.

In his 1953 book, *Catfishin'*, Joe Mathers called bullhead baits "excellent, especially for large catfish."

"Use small living forms, three to six inches long," he wrote. "Snip off the barbels, spines, and dorsal fin causing the fish to bleed and

Small bullheads have been used to entice big catfish for decades. They're tough and easy to keep alive.

flounder in the water. They are very tough, easy to keep alive and excellent for use on trot or other set lines. Small bullheads can usually be taken in great numbers with a seine or on hook and line from backwaters, bayous, ponds, and small lakes and streams . . ."

Georgia writer Jeff Samsel, an avid catfisherman, reports that channel cats sometimes are used for bait, as well. "For big flathead catfish, many long-time river fishermen contend there is no better bait than another catfish," he tells me. "Bullheads and channel cats are most commonly used, but whatever kind of catfish a flathead is accustomed to seeing in a waterway is probably the best cat to use as bait in that location. Any cat up to a couple pounds will do. Hook the bait in the back toward the tail, and suspend it just off the bottom."

Sometimes you can rig the bait just by catching it. When Dorothy Taylor of Fort Scott, Kansas, cleaned a fifty-three-pound flathead she caught, she found a one-and-a-half-pound channel cat in its belly. The channel cat, not the flathead, had her hook in its mouth.

Other Wacky Baits

John Phillips tells a story about a friend, out of bait, who resorted to using a roadkill possum on his hook. It worked. "I was very surprised," his friend said. "The catfish hit the possum bait better than they had the cut shad, live minnows, and worms I had been using."

"Some people say adding WD-40 or Preparation H to lures and bait brings added success," said Vince Travnichek in an article published in the *Missouri Conservationist*. The explanation is that both contain shark oil, which attracts fish. The manufacturer of WD-40 said that shark oil is not an ingredient in the product, but the manufacturer of Preparation H stated that their product contained 3 percent shark liver oil. Both said they had heard of these angling secrets but did not recommend using their products in such a manner."

Anglers in some areas say bubble gum can be a very effective cat-catcher.

James Patterson of Mississippi River Guide Service in Bartlett, Tennessee, says he has caught catfish using mulberries, bologna, and crickets and has cleaned cats that had such items as fried potatoes and pork chops in their bellies. "The most unusual thing I've found in a catfish was bubble gum," he notes. "I landed the fish, and it was squirting pink liquid everywhere. When I cut it open, it still had three full pieces of bubble gum inside."

Some anglers actually use bubble gum for bait. "We use Bazooka, Double Bubble, and Bubble Yum," a Georgia catfisherman told me. "They all catch cats so long as you chew the gum a little before baiting your hook. Don't chew all the flavor out, though, or they won't take it."

The wackiest cat bait? No bait at all. Jug fishermen on the White and Mississippi rivers in Arkansas catch channel and blue cats using only a gold crappie hook dangled beneath each jug. "Catfish see that flashy gold hook and grab it," one told me. "You don't need bait at all."

This just goes to prove what I've been saying all along: sooner or later you'll catch a catfish no matter what you dangle in the water. And that, my friend, is one of the things that makes catfishing so much fun.

"Grocery Store" Baits

As their name implies, grocery store baits can be purchased at your local supermarket. Among these are enticements such as shrimp, cheese, hot dogs, dog food, bread, bacon, and even squid.

Both fresh and frozen shrimp can be used to entice blue, channel, and flathead cats up to about ten pounds. Run your hook from the head of the shrimp out through the tail, and leave the hook point exposed.

Cheese is an ingredient in many stinkbait concoctions, especially smelly cheeses such as Limburger. In some areas, however, anglers simply use chunks of sharp cheddar or Velveeta, both of which are said to be effective cat catchers.

On South Carolina's Santee-Cooper lakes, hallowed water for catfish fans, hot dogs are used to entice cats—but not just any hot dogs. "They don't like all-beef hot dogs," one guide told me. "But they love the cheap kind made out of chicken or turkey." And you thought catfish weren't discriminating diners!

Will cats eat dog food? Indeed. Cat men in Mississippi, Tennessee, and Alabama swear Tender Chunks is head and shoulders above the rest. But an angler in Arkansas claims Kibbles and Bits is tops for small channel cats.

Bread doesn't seem like a great cat bait, but I once watched a tour guide mash an entire loaf into a big dough ball then drop it over the side of the boat into the clear waters of Silver Springs, Florida. One of the biggest cats I ever saw came up and swallowed the entire loaf of bread in a single gulp. Might be worth trying.

Massachusetts catter Roger Aziz has caught more line-class-record white cats than anyone. His favorite bait? Bacon. "Hickory-smoked bacon works best," he says. "Always."

In winter, when live baits are hard to come by, anglers must rely more on various types of grocery baits. Randle Hall, a Texas catfish guide told me, "I started experimenting and found that squid really works. I use noncleaned squid bought at a supermarket, half a squid per hook."

Advanced Tactics

Cats in the Woods

In the eyes of many, flooded spring woods are the best catfishing spots bar none.

When I first saw the spring crawfish run, as my friend Jim Spencer calls it, the sight astounded me. I've witnessed this incredible natural phenomenon several times in the intervening years, but memories of my first run will always be most vivid.

Spring floodwaters were receding along Arkansas's lower White River, and when the river fell to the right level on the Clarendon gauge, Jim phoned.

"We need to go tomorrow," he said, "or they'll be gone. I'll pick you up at five a.m."

We met at the appointed time—Jim, me, and my son Josh—and drove to the river. After motoring a few miles downstream in a john-boat, we tied the craft to some old cypress steps on the river bank then made our way up and walked to a small oxbow off the beaten path. A bit of water still flowed through the run-outs connecting the river and oxbow lake, but in a day or so as the water continued falling, the connection between river and lake would be severed.

Only days before, the woods around the lake had been inundated beneath twelve to eighteen inches of water, the result of high water that

When floodplain woodlands are inundated by river overflows, catfish anglers may have to move into backwater areas off the river proper to find their quarry.

comes on average three years out of five. As the White River dropped, however, the water was pulled out, leaving behind muddy, leaf-strewn ground. But even now, with the water gone, the ground was hard to see, for thousands upon thousands of crayfish covered the damp earth. You couldn't step without mashing them beneath your feet, huge rusty-red crustaceans with pincers like Maine lobsters.

"Look, Dad!" Josh exclaimed. "They're everywhere! There must be a million of them!"

We had toted a one-hundred-quart cooler to the lake's edge, and each of us carried a wire fish basket in which to place our catch. Walking through the woods, we gathered crawfish—a dozen here, a dozen there—and when our baskets were full, we returned to the cooler and dumped the catch in. Little yelps emanated from the collection crew whenever a crawfish found its mark with those big pincers, but in less than an hour, the cooler was overflowing.

"This is the best of two worlds," Jim said. "We've got catfish bait and dinner, too, all in one cooler."

The catfish liked the crawfish almost as much as we did. That night, fishing with crawfish tails in the run-out between river and lake, each of us caught a dozen or more cats, and before the sun rose, the three of us had polished off more than ten pounds apiece of spicy, fresh-boiled crawfish apiece. I decided then and there that catfish, crawdads, and bottomland rivers form a minor trinity.

Woods Fishing

I had known for years that catfish migrate into flooded spring woods to eat crawfish. As a youngster, I often accompanied uncles on woods-fishing junkets, tying yo-yos and limblines to green branches along the edges of inundated forests and baiting them with the tails of crawfish caught in homemade dip nets. As we'd paddle through the woods making our sets, big cats would shoot this way and that, spooked by our approach. We'd see their wakes, sometimes the tip of a fin or tail, as they scurried away through the shallow water. By that sign, we knew our timing was right. Cats were in the woods gorging on the annual banquet nature provided, and by morning, we'd be weary from catching and cleaning catfish.

There was no doubt about the inspiration for this catfish celebration. The fish we caught—blues, channels, and flatheads—were literally stuffed to the gills with crawfish. Often, a fish would take our bait even though several crawfish could be seen protruding from its gullet. Their stomachs were distended like beer bellies with dozens and dozens of crawfish. Eating more was an impossibility but still they tried.

Woods fishing is one of the oldest yet most obscure forms of catfishing. Few cat fans are familiar with the tactic today, but earlier this century, it was widely practiced in the lower Mississippi River Valley. D.S. Jordan and B.W. Evermann were among the first to write about this unique sport in their 1923 book, *American Food and Game Fishes*.

"During the spring rise in the Mississippi, hundreds of square miles of the adjacent country become flooded, and then the catfish leave the rivers, lakes, and bayous, and 'take to the woods,'" they said. "Here the fishermen follow them, and 'woods' or 'swamp' fishing is resorted to. Short 'brush' lines with single hooks are tied to limbs of trees here and there through the forest, in such a way as to allow the hook to hang about six inches under water. The trees selected are usually those along the edges of the 'float' roads, and, that he may readily find his lines again, the fisherman ties a white rag to each tree to which he has attached a line.

"The lines are visited daily, or as often as practicable, and the fish are placed in a live-box, where they are kept until the tugboats from Morgan City (Louisiana) make their regular collecting trips. Then they are transferred to very large live-boxes or cars carried in tow by the tugs, and are taken to Morgan City, where the fish are dressed, put in barrels with ice, and shipped to the retailers in many States of the Union."

In *Catfishin'*, published in 1953, Joe Mathers also commented.

"Brush line fishing (also referred to as 'woods' or 'swamp' fishing) is employed by fisherman along the Mississippi and its large tributaries," he writes. "As the spring floods come, these rivers overflow their banks and flood the surrounding lowlands. The blue catfish especially characteristically leaves the rivers, lakes, and bayous and moves into these flooded areas. The fishermen follow them . . ."

Gorging on Crayfish

Because the ground in a river floodplain is low and flat, a rise in river level of only a few

Catfish egg production in floodplain-river ecosystems is enhanced by the presence of numerous terrestrial crayfish during years of high water. Catfish caught during this time may be literally stuffed with these high-protein crustaceans.

inches can flood literally thousands of acres of bottoms. As the water rises and the woodlands become flooded, a new food source—terrestrial crayfish—becomes available to catfish.

Crayfish are extremely abundant in most bottomland hardwood forests, but during most of the year they live on land and are inaccessible to catfish. During overflow periods, however, the crayfish are forced to live in an aquatic environment, and catfish are drawn to them like kids to a candy store. Flatheads, blues, and channel cats all join the feeding frenzy, moving from rivers, lakes, bayous, and sloughs into the shallow water that now inundates many acres of bottoms. They will feed here as long as the water is high enough to swim in, sometimes for several months.

The Limbliner's Season

It would seem with so many actively feeding fish gathered in shallow water, it would be easy to catch them. But that is not the case. Fishing in flooded woods is difficult in the best of circumstances, and because the catfish are widely scattered and have an enormous supply of natural food, catching them on rod and reel is iffy.

Catching them with setlines is another story. This is the limbliners' season, and as soon as the bottoms are inundated, their fun begins. Setlines hung from low branches produce extraordinary numbers of catfish, particularly toward the end of flood season when the waters are warm.

Some limbliners make special sets with a piece of rubber inner tube tied in the middle of each line to act as a shock absorber that prevents catfish from pulling free. Others tie their sets on springy green limbs that function in a similar manner. Still others fish with yo-yos, the spring-wound Autofisher rigs popular in many parts of the South. Dozens of sets may

Limblines can be set individually at strategic fishing spots to catch catfish feeding in flooded woods.

be placed, and each is checked at regular intervals to remove the catch. This is an extraordinary time characterized by extraordinary fishing.

Run-outs and Run-off

If you're a die-hard rod-and-reel angler, you'll want to pay particular attention to the part of this phenomenon known as "the run-off." This occurs when a river "falls out of" a connected oxbow, usually in spring or early summer when overflow waters recede from the river bottoms. There comes a point when the water has fallen low enough that the only connections between an oxbow and its parent stream are small chutes or "run-outs" created by low points in the area topography. In some cases, only one run-out exists; in others, there are several. All run-outs, however, serve up extraordinary catfishing for savvy anglers.

A live crawfish or crawfish tail drifted through a run-out area is an irresistible enticement for cats in the woods.

The key to run-out fishing is timing. The best fishing will be during the few days before the river falls completely out of the lake. Water constricted in the run-out chutes increases in velocity. Crawfish and other forage animals are pulled by the current into the rushing stream of water and adjacent areas. When this happens, catfish gather in great numbers to gorge on the resulting feast. Some hold near cover at the head of the run-out in the lake. Others position themselves at the run-out's tail where the rushing water meets the river. All feed ravenously while the bounty is before them, and any bait—crawfish, night crawlers, cutbait, live fish—drifted through or along the run-out area is likely to be taken.

A float rig works great here with the bobber positioned so the bait floats just off the bottom. Cast above the run-out, and let the rig drift back through, or drift the rig through the current in the run-out tail. Live crawfish or crawfish tails are top baits in this situation, for rod-and-reel and setline fishing. But because these prespawn catfish are feeding ravenously, they'll accept almost any offering from night crawlers and chicken liver to live bluegills and cutbait.

Big blue cats such as this often feed in the run-out connecting an oxbow lake to its parent river.

For run-out fishing to be successful, you'll have to learn the river-gauge level at which the parent river will overflow into each oxbow. When gauge numbers are higher than this number, you know the river and oxbow are connected. When gauge numbers are lower than the "magic" number, the river level is so low it doesn't flow into the lake. Run-off conditions exist when the river level is just slightly higher than the magic number, and it is during the few days when this occurs that run-out catfishing is at its best.

The best way to obtain the "magic" gauge number is to inquire at local bait shops or ask area anglers. You then can read the current gauge number in local newspapers or by calling government hotlines to plan a trip during peak periods.

Although the popularity of woods fishing has declined in recent decades, this is still a top-

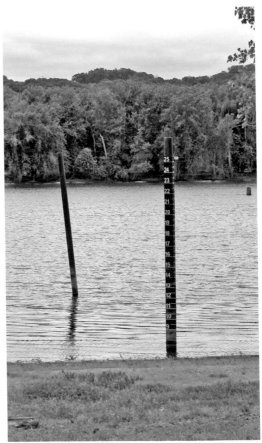

River gauges provide important water-level information needed by those who fish run-outs between oxbow lakes and rivers.

notch tactic for catching lots of catfish, big and small. If you live in the lower Mississippi River Valley or anywhere else these floodplain-river ecosystems exist, give woods fishing a try this spring when the big rivers have overflowed their banks. When catfish are in the woods, it's a sure bet they'll be biting.

Scientific Evidence and Big River Conservation

Fishermen have known for decades that catfish feed heavily on crawfish in floodplain-river ecosystems, such as those found in the lower Mississippi Valley, but only in recent years have fisheries researchers studied this phenomenon. Don Jackson and Joe Flotemersch, researchers at Mississippi State University, studied the unique relationship between terrestrially burrowing crayfish and channel cats in channelized and non-channelized sections of Mississippi's Yockanookany River. Some of what they learned is old news to ardent woods anglers. For example, they found that "adult channel catfish aggregated in locations where the river channel and adjacent floodplain were coupled and subsequently foraged heavily on these crayfish." Sound familiar? It should. This is the typical run-out fishing scenario described in this chapter.

The most important information discovered during this study was not previously known. Jackson and Flotemersch learned that peak use of crayfish occurs prior to egg occurrence in channel catfish. And because the crayfish are excellent sources of essential amino acids and essential fatty acids, they are likely to be significant resources for egg development. In other words, if the rivers didn't overflow and the catfish couldn't reach the crayfish to feed on them, the catfish would not produce as many eggs. As a result, these floodplain-river ecosystems would not produce the astounding numbers of healthy cats now available for anglers to catch.

For this reason, all of us who enjoy catfishing in big bottomland river ecosystems should be concerned about flood-control and navigation projects that utilize channelization, dredging, and construction of levees and wing dikes. Such activities can "disconnect" floodplains and rivers and hurt catfish stock.

Woods Fishing Tips

- Big boats are practically useless when fishing flooded timber. Most woods fishermen opt for a lightweight narrow johnboat they can maneuver through the trees.

- Carry hip boots or waders because the best fishing spots may be unreachable except on foot.

- In the close confines around run-outs, use a five-and-a-half- to six-foot medium-heavy rod with a whippy tip and stout butt section. This will allow you to flip a bait in just the right spot with fewer hang-ups.

- If catfish seem persnickety, try peeling crawfish tails before putting them on a hook.

- Always practice selective harvest. Keep a few small cats to eat; release the big ones. Better yet, eat the bait. Crawfish are delicious!

- Know the fishing regulations where you fish before using setlines or other such tackle. On border rivers between two states, be sure you're properly licensed.

Tailwater Tactics

Zero in on the fast water below a big-river dam for blue-ribbon catfish action.

Catfish live in big reservoirs. You can find them in many smaller lakes. They swim in the long open stretches of our rivers and streams. But if you're fishing on your own and want to increase your odds for success, if you want to be catching fish instead of just fishing, drive to the nearest cat river and follow it upstream to the first dam. In that tumbling, foamy-white mass of fast-moving water right below the dam, you'll find them—cats as long as your leg, at least. You'll have to land one exceeding seventy-five pounds before you'll draw much notice in some tailwaters, but that's always a distinct possibility if you know your stuff.

Focus on the first mile or two of water below the dam. Study it. Fish it. Get to know it on intimate terms—every rock, every hole, every hump, every dike, every nuance of cover and current. And if you play the game right and Lady Luck is on your side, sooner or later you'll hook what will probably be the biggest fish you've ever battled in freshwater—a trophy-class cat.

The churning water below a dam creates conditions big catfish find much to their liking.

Why Tailwaters?

Catfish are drawn to tailwaters by an urge to procreate. As days grow longer and water warms, cats leave deep wintering holes and begin upstream runs toward spawning areas. Before dams were built, the only things interrupting this annual procession were natural barriers, such as shoals, log jams, and the like. Today, however, the runs usually are stopped short by dams.

This wouldn't concern catfishermen if spawning was all cats had on their minds. Upon encountering a dam, the fish would simply turn back to find spawning grounds. But that's not the case. With these fish, eating precedes breeding. And at every dam on every river, there's a banquet awaiting them.

Baitfish like shad and skipjack herring are especially plentiful. Some are washed from above

and wind up crippled or dead after passing through turbines. Cats gather like kids around an ice-cream truck, gobbling every morsel that swims or drifts near.

Most catfish remain in the tailwater for days or weeks, gorging 'round-the-clock on the irresistible feast. But in the end, nature can't be ignored. Most catfish eventually move downriver to spawning areas. As some leave, though, others arrive. And if conditions remain good— if water flow is ample to maintain high oxygen levels and attract schools of baitfish—those that leave will return after spawning, staying as long as they're comfortable and well fed. Thus, fishing for cats remains excellent through several months from late spring through summer.

Tailwater Hotspots

To better understand the catfishing dynamics of a tailwater, it helps to divide the tailwater into three sections: 1) the whitewater reach, which is the uppermost portion of the tailwater near the dam and adjacent structures; 2) the middle reach, which begins where churning water from the dam starts smoothing out and slowing down; and 3) the downstream reach, which begins where man-made structures are replaced by natural habitat. Each section's length and breadth may vary considerably depending on the type of dam and the river's size, but all sections are easily identified, and each offers different types of structure and cover attractive to cats under differing conditions. Learn what to look for, and you'll improve your odds of hooking a big cat.

The Whitewater Reach

From late spring through summer, this section of the tailwater serves up the best action for trophy catfish. Current velocity, baitfish abundance, and oxygen content reach their highest levels here—conditions big catfish find much drags your bait slowly across the bottom. Cast toward the dam and into the head of a groove, letting the rig sink. If you've hit the groove properly, your bait should stop—for a moment at least—as soon as it hits bottom. If you missed the groove, you'll feel the bait tumbling along at a fast clip. Practice enables you to know for sure what's happening.

When you hit the groove, allow your bait to remain in one spot as long as possible. Cats swim back and forth from one end of the cone-shaped groove to the other over and over again. The grooves are usually short—fifty feet or fewer—so it won't take long for a cat to find your bait. When one does, its strike will be hard and unmistakable. Drop your rod tip toward the cat when it hits, then set the hook.

If cats quit biting in one groove, reposition your boat in a similar location and try again. Water flow through a dam increases or decreases as power requirements or water levels demand. So even though water runs continuously, the flow may change several times daily. When the flow changes, cats often move and search out more slack water in which to feed.

The washout hole is another important catfishing area in the whitewater reach. This is a depression scoured in the river bottom by the forceful action of water released from the dam. In most cases, it starts at the dam face and extends downstream for a few to many yards. If safety factors permit, use sonar to pinpoint the downstream lip of the hole where most cats hold. This will appear as a sharp drop discernible as you move toward the dam. If the washout hole is within the danger zone off limits to boaters, you'll have to speculate on its position and fish it from a distance.

A jig/cutbait combo works great in this situation. Impale a chunk of cutbait on a heavy leadhead. Motor upstream as far as safety per-

When fishing the whitewater reach, look for catfish holding in the "grooves" of slower-moving water between openings in the dam.

to their liking. As upstream spawning migrations progress, catfish crowd into the food-rich water immediately below the dam in ever-increasing numbers with larger fish laying claim to most prime feeding locations.

Many jumbo catfish hold in the "grooves" or "current tunnels" of slower-moving water between openings in the dam. When water is released, the fastest flow is in the center of the discharge, and the slowest water is on the outer edges of the flow. All surface water appears to move at the same speed, but the area of water between two discharges—the groove or tunnel—is actually slower-moving water where cats usually hold. Fishing these grooves is more productive than fishing the main current.

Chunks of cutbait are the perfect enticement in this situation. Slice a shad, herring, or sucker into one-inch chunks. Larger pieces are difficult to present properly in the current. Push the hook once through the bait, leaving the point exposed to ensure a good hookset.

A basic three-way rig with a Kahle hook and bell sinker works great in this situation. The sinker should be heavy enough so the current mits, then drop the bait to the bottom and crank it up a bit. As your boat drifts, use your motor to maintain a speed that keeps your line vertical below you. When you reach the downstream lip of the washout hole, the bait will start moving up the drop and dragging behind the boat. This is when most strikes occur. If you get one, great. If not, continue drifting until you're on the shelf below the hole, then reel up your rig, motor upstream, and drift through again.

It's important to remember that constant water flow through the dam is necessary to maintain good catfishing conditions in the whitewater reach. Should conditions exist that force dam operators to close all gates, catfishing success will take a nosedive until ample water flow is restored. The best catfishing generally coincides with periods of highest water flow when most or all gates are open.

Remember, too, the best catfishing locales in a tailwater are easily "fished out," especially toward either end of the prime late-spring/summer fishing period. You may catch dozens of catfish in the hotspots you identify one day then return to the same fishing areas on several consecutive days and not catch a single fish. If this happens, fish other sections of the tailwater while allowing a period of rejuvenation. Catfish from other reaches will eventually move in to repopulate prime feeding areas.

The Middle Reach
Moving downstream from the washout hole, you'll soon enter the middle reach, a stretch of calmer water where man-made structures, such as wing dikes and riprap, are still prevalent. A few cats, especially smaller fish, inhabit this section throughout the warm months, but trophy action peaks during short periods of reduced water flow through the dam. If one or several gates are closed, cats feeding in the whitewater reach often move to middle reach

Trophy cats often hold near wing dikes, which are some of the most prevalent structures in the middle reach of a tailwater.

structures that attract schools of baitfish. They continue feeding here until water flow is restored to higher levels, drawing them away.

Wing dikes are the predominant cat structure in this part of the tailwater. These long narrow rock structures direct current into the main channel to lessen shoreline erosion.

Most actively feeding catfish hold near the river's bottom on a wing dike's upstream side. Reduced current exists in this area along the length of the dike, allowing cats to remain active without expending excess energy while feeding. Some active catfish feed along the crown and in the boil-line over and just downstream from the wing dike's crown. When resting, cats move to deeper scour holes, usually near the end of the dike. Occasionally these fish are enticed to bite but only when bait is presented right under their nose.

Bottom-fishing often is productive here, but a slip-bobber rig allows you to cover more water quickly. Position the bobber stop so the float suspends your bait just above the river bottom. Add enough weight to hold the bait down and stand the bobber up, then let the rig drift into eddies and pockets of calm water along the dike. Tease the rig around the rocks, easing it alongside drift piles and other catfish-attracting cover. If nothing happens after you've worked an area thoroughly, move your bobber stop down the line and drift through shallower. Or move to another dike and try again.

Humps and boulders in the middle reach also merit attention. Those with shallow crowns may be visible or at least apparent due to the boil-line above them. Sonar may be needed to find those in deeper water.

Fish these structures as you would a wing dike. Most feeding cats are near bottom on the upstream edge with a few feeding near the crown and boil-line areas. Cats in slack water behind boulders and humps are usually inactive.

The Downstream Reach
You eventually reach a point below the dam where the river starts looking natural again.

The mouth of a tributary is a prime place to seek catfish in the downstream reach of a tailwater. Catfish will be more concentrated in this portion of the tailwater when water conditions in the whitewater and middle reach are poor.

The channel begins meandering once more, trees have toppled in, cutbanks reappear, and the hand of man is less in evidence. This is the downstream reach of the tailwater.

When conditions in upper sections of the tailwater are ideal, the downstream reach may be almost devoid of large cats. But all catfish pass through this area at least twice each year during upstream and downstream migrations, and if conditions in the whitewater reach become unfavorable for extended periods in late spring and summer, catfish may frequent portions downstream for weeks on end.

Tributaries are important hotspots in this section. Cats ascend tributaries to spawn, and they congregate at tributary mouths during prespawn and postspawn periods. If the mouth of the feeder stream is deep at its confluence with the river or if the tributary channel joins the main river channel, the area also may have exceptional potential during winter when cats tend to gather in deep water near channel breaks. During summer, if a tributary brings a cool, well-oxygenated inflow to the river, catfish may move in if dam releases upstream are slight or nil.

Proper timing is the key to success when fishing here, but tributaries always merit a look when catfishing is unproductive in upstream reaches.

Other prime fishing areas in the downstream reach are the same you might find on any river: undercut banks and timbered holes in outside bends; deep-water chutes; bridge channels; rock, gravel, and sand bars; log jams; side channels connecting the main river with backwaters and oxbows; and so forth.

Study the tailwater each time you fish. Ask yourself where cats are most likely to be. If it's late spring or summer and there's lots of

Dam tailwaters have produced some of the largest catfish ever taken in the United States, but to fish a tailwater effectively, the catfisherman must know where his quarry is likely to be based on water conditions and other factors.

water flowing from the dam, the whitewater reach likely will produce the most action. If water releases have been temporarily halted, the middle reach may be your best bet. You'll find some cats in upper reaches of the tailwater in autumn, winter, and early spring, but you'll probably do better around tributaries and other prime fishing locales in the downstream reach. Adjust your fishing tactics as necessary to capitalize on each situation.

You may not break any records next time you fish for tailwater catfish. But if you employ the right tactics under the right conditions, you're almost sure to catch plenty of eating-sized catfish, and every time you return, there's always the chance you'll tie into a real record breaker. They're out there now swimming in the tailwaters.

Fishing from Shore

Many tailwater anglers fish from shore. Unfortunately, the shore angler faces distinct disadvantages. Pinpointing casts to distant catfish-holding structures is more difficult and current billows your line, dragging your rig out of position. Fighting big fish is more difficult and time-consuming. Anglers may be crowded together, leading to tangles and tussles.

Shore fishing can be productive, however, if you use proper equipment. Use a long rod—a ten- to fourteen-foot surf-casting rod is ideal—to achieve greater distance on your casts. Holding the rod tip high minimizes the amount of line in the water for better bait presentation, and it also lessens your chance of getting tangled with lines of nearby fishermen. Normal spinning and bait-casting reels both work fine, but you'll achieve longer casts with a good heavy-duty spinning reel. Use nothing less than thirty-pound-test line when targeting big catfish.

Carry plenty of rig components, such as sinkers and jigheads. You'll lose many.

Let your rig settle then get it to hold. But don't leave it in one spot more than a few minutes. Move the bait again to be sure it hasn't tumbled into a hole where cats can't find it.

Safety First

Tailwater catfishermen should be aware of safety considerations at all times. When dam gates are opened, sudden rises in water can be dangerous.

Tailwaters have Jekyll-and-Hyde personalities. One minute a tailwater is peaceful, calm, and easygoing. But in the blink of an eye, it can turn into a raging, out-of-control monster that seems intent on your destruction.

Safety should be foremost on your mind whenever fishing a tailwater. Wear a life jacket every minute you're there. Maintain a safe and legal distance from the dam. Avoid anchoring, if possible, and if you do anchor, use a quick-release tie-off that will let you cut loose in a heartbeat. Keep a knife handy just in case.

Learn the warning signals—sirens, flashing lights, etc.—that indicate impending sudden releases from the dam. Keep your motor in top working order. Watch for boulders, inundated wing dikes, and other structures that can cause you to capsize.

Remember, catching a big cat is never worth risking your life or the lives of others.

Mountain Stream Catfishing

Highland streams often harbor impressive populations of catfish.

Despite popular misconceptions, cool, clear mountain streams offer outstanding catfishing. Proof is found in *Fish Arkansas*, a brochure listing the types of fish found in twenty-four of the Natural State's cold- and cool-water streams. All but one of these waters was identified as having healthy populations of channel catfish. All but two have good numbers of flathead catfish. Blue catfish were listed as residents in nine. No other fish, not even trout or smallmouth bass, inhabit more of Arkansas's mountain streams than catfish.

This same situation exists in many states, and the savvy angler can catch plenty of cats when conditions are right. Especially helpful is a knowledge of the rapids, holes, and pools found in most mountain streams and the ways catfish relate to each structure.

The cool, clear waters of mountain streams aren't often considered prime catfishing hotspots, but these waters frequently serve up superb fishing for big flatheads, blues, and channel cats.

Rapids

Rapids, or riffles, form over hard bottoms and are shallower than other spots because water can't erode the hard substrate. Water flow is constricted here, making it move forcefully. You can see rapids because water boils up here creating haystacks and whitecaps.

Holes

Holes form below rapids. The bottom softens here, and the rapids' churning water scours it away, leaving a depression several yards long.

Pools

Below each hole, the current slows. Sediments fall, the downstream end of the hole gets shallower, and a pool forms. Pools have no significant depth changes. They may extend a mile or more depending on bottom composition and river size. But when the water encounters another area of hard bottom, rapids form again, and the sequence starts anew—rapids, hole, pool.

Of these three structures, holes typically harbor the most catfish. Cats travel through rapids and pools when moving and sometimes visit these areas to feed. They seldom stay long, however. Holes, on the other hand, provide depth, current, food, and security. The hole's deepest portion is the den or bedroom area where cats rest out of the current. The upper end is the kitchen or dining room where cats usually feed.

Rocks, logs, and other cover in a hole's deeper upstream end are especially attractive to actively feeding fish. Cats ambush prey from behind these current breaks. Cover objects where current is lighter or water is shallower aren't as likely to hold active catfish.

A bobber/drift presentation proves the undoing of many mountain stream cats.

Wade Fishing

One excellent mountain-stream fishing technique is wading and casting to fish-holding structure and cover. If the stream isn't too deep, a bobber/drift presentation works well. Position the bobber so the bait hangs just above the bottom. Add enough weight to hold the bait down, then drift the rig alongside cover and structures. With practice, you'll become adept at steering the bait past holding areas without worrying about hang-ups.

A drift presentation is still appropriate in deeper water, but dispense with the bobber and add just enough lead so the bait still bounces along in the current. To rig, slip an egg sinker on your line, and eighteen inches above the bait, add a barrel swivel to hold the egg sinker in place.

Good bait choices include crayfish, night crawlers, minnows, creek chubs, hellgrammites, grasshoppers, salamanders, and frogs.

Mountain streams are hotbeds for untold numbers of fat sassy catfish. It may seem unusual fishing for cats outside the mosquito-infested bottomlands you normally visit, but it's a change of pace you're sure to enjoy.

Finessing Big-River Cats

One of the country's top cat guides shares a technique for catching cats in flowing water.

If you ever catfish on the Tennessee River in Hardin County, Tennessee, you're liable to run into a charming fellow from Corinth, Mississippi, named Phil "The Little Catman" King. Phil practically lives on the stretch of river between Pickwick and Kentucky lakes. He's a well-known personality in these parts for at least two reasons: 1) he's a nationally renowned catfish guide, often written about, and often seen on TV fishing shows, and 2) he's won more catfishing tournaments than perhaps any man alive, including the World Championship of Catfishing and the Cabela's King Kat Classic.

I had the pleasure of fishing with Phil and learned a catfishing tactic you could probably apply successfully on almost any big catfish river. It's basically a way of bottom-bouncing baits as you drift, but it's not quite as simple as that description makes it sound. To me, it's a form of "finesse fishing." The angler must develop a keen "feel" for his bait rig to keep in the fish zone without getting hung up.

Rig Right

Let's start with Phil's rigging. This consists of six main components: a three-way swivel, a barrel swivel, a two-ounce bell sinker, two 5/0 Daiichi Circle-Wide Bleeding Bait hooks, and fishing line—sixty-five-pound Berkley Whiplash braid for the main line braid and

Mississippi catfish guide Phil King uses specialized "finesse" tactics to catch big stringers of river catfish.

sixty-pound Big Game mono off the three-way swivel. The rig is baited with one of two baits: a big bloody chunk of fresh chicken liver or what Phil describes as a "catfish sandwich." The latter is simply the innards of a big skipjack herring sandwiched between two side fillets from the same baitfish.

Presentation

The rig is presented in deep river holes, some dropping below seventy feet. Phil starts at the head of a hole and drifts through after the bait rig has been lowered to the bottom. Most cats hold beside river-bottom timber and rocks, which "telegraph" signals through the braided line to the angler above. The angler must be attentive at all times, raising or lowering the rig with the rod tip so he maintains "feel" with the rig below and keeps it bouncing across the pieces of cover and structures without hanging up.

While drifting, Phil watches a fish finder, looking for signals indicating cats holding near structures below. If he spies good fish that fails to take the bait on the first drift, he may drift through the hole again, targeting those spots that appeared to hold catfish once more.

During the four hours my son Josh and I fished with Phil using this method, we caught scores of blue and channel cats in the five- to twelve-pound range. Bigger specimens eluded us, but

Phil King (right) and the author's son, Josh Sutton, with a nice mess of channel and blue cats caught while "finesse fishing" in the Tennessee River.

Phil has landed blue cats and flatheads up to fifty pounds using this tactic. For the big river angler hoping to catch numbers of cats with an occasional trophy-class fish in the mix, this is a superb technique that's easy to learn.

Wing Dikes and Eddies

On navigable waterways, fishing long rock dikes is the way to success.

The long rock wall jutted from the shore out into the Mississippi River. At the wall's end, the river rolled around on itself to create a huge vortex. It looked like someone had pulled a huge plug from the river bottom and all the water was going down an enormous drain.

We called such maelstroms suckholes when I was a youngster trotlining the river with older relatives. Some call them "whirlpools." James Patterson of Mississippi River Guide Service prefers the term "eddy."

"Drop your bait right at the edge of that eddy," Patterson said, "and free-spool it all the way to the bottom." I did as he suggested, and to my surprise, the big chunk of shad went straight down. The instant the bait touched bottom, before I was quite prepared, something huge grabbed it. And when it did, that something huge nearly snatched the rod from my hands.

I never saw that something huge. It got the best of me, as the big ones often do. I'm quite certain, however, it was a catfish—probably a sizeable blue. And I learned that day that catfish fans who often fish large navigable waterways should study and understand both structures Patterson and I were fishing: wing dikes and eddies.

Wing Dike Facts

The rock walls known as wing dikes are placed in strategic locations to help maintain ship-channel depth and lessen shoreline erosion. They are most numerous in hydropower and navigation dam tailwaters but may be scattered along the entire length of a big river. They fulfill their intended functions by diverting the current. They usually lay perpendicular to shore, and when moving water strikes one, it swirls back on itself. The force of the current then moves outward toward the middle of the river. The water velocity slows, allowing suspended sediments to fall and accumulate on the river bottom.

Inactive catfish typically stay on a wing dike's downstream side lying on the bottom, usually near inshore reaches. Current is minimal here, so rest is possible.

Tennessee catfishing guide James Patterson often catches trophy catfish in the swirling waters around Mississippi River wing dams.

Catfish Positioning on Wing Dikes

Most feeding catfish, especially the more numerous small cats, hold near the river's bottom on a wing dike's upstream side. The reason for this is three-fold. First, water hydraulics here create a "tube" of reduced current near the bottom running the length of the dike. Hungry cats can feed here without using excess energy. Also, this is an abundant food zone with crayfish and mussels in the rocks and shad, herring, and other baitfish holding in the slower cylinder of water. Finally, when the river's high and the wing dike is submerged, catfish can feed on addled or injured forage animals easily captured in the boil-line directly above the rocks and immediately downstream.

You should now understand the basics of wing dike catfishing: to catch lots of eating-sized cats, fish the upstream side. Downstream is rarely as productive.

There is another lesson, however, perhaps even more important: trophy catfish—blues, channels, and flatheads—are best targeted around the eddies near the ends of wing dikes. This I learned from James Patterson, who often fishes around these whirlpools with his clients and who frequently catches monster cats when doing so.

"I don't fish the eddy part of this rotation," Patterson told me the day I hooked something huge. "Instead, I fish the current along the edges. I find that catfish in eddy water are not active. Active cats are along the edges, so that's where I want to anchor and fish."

Baits, Rigs, and Tactics

Like most ardent blue-cat anglers, Patterson relies on two primary baits to entice his quarry. "I use live shad a lot, even though they're hard

James Patterson (right) nets a nice Mississippi River blue cat author Keith Sutton hooked while fishing near a wing dike.

An eddy, or whirlpool, forming at the end of a wing dike. Bait dropped adjacent to this swirling bit of water will sink quickly to the bottom, where it's sure to entice any nearby cat.

to find," he says. "Cut skipjack herrings also are good bait."

A simple three-way-swivel rig is Patterson's standard. The two-foot hook leader is tipped with a 3/0 to 7/0 Eagle Claw Kahle hook. The eight-inch weight leader is tied to a three-ounce sinker. His fishing gear consists of "a heavy-action casting rod with a light tip and a lot of butt strength" and a bait-casting reel that holds at least 200 yards of twenty-pound-test line.

"I anchor above the hole I intend to fish," Patterson says, "then cast to the spot and let the reel free-spool until the weight hits bottom. Sometimes I'll have out two hundred feet of line. Blues usually hit hard and quick, so rod holders are necessary if you fish more rods than you can hold."

It would seem that a bait tossed to the edge of one of these huge suckholes would swirl a round and a round. But when done properly, the bait will sink quickly to the bottom and remain stationary. Reposition your rig if necessary to achieve this end, then prepare for the rod-jarring strike that will soon follow if a giant cat is nearby. Often, big cats cruise slowly through a hole waiting for something to jolt their taste buds before they rush in to strike. Allow the bait to sit up to ten minutes, but if there's no bite by then, move and try another eddy hole.

Strikes usually come quick and hard, so use heavy tackle and keep a firm grip on your rod at all times. One moment of inattention could cost you the catfish of lifetime. I learned that lesson the hard way when my "something huge" got away.

Jungle Cats

When cats are hiding in heavy cover, you have to move in with them to enjoy success.

O n lakes with little fishing pressure, thick cover doesn't seem to hold any more large catfish than other, more easy-to-fish areas. But on heavily fished lakes, there seems to be a definite correlation between big cats and woody tangles.

There are two primary reasons for this. First, common sense says catfish don't get big by frequenting heavily fished haunts. Most heavyweights get that way by living in out of the way home sites where most anglers don't dare to

venture. That's why they haven't already been caught.

Second, big catfish instinctively prefer the protection of heavy cover. Outsized cats are extremely wary and angler-shy, and this contributes to their natural tendency to hide in the most concealed places possible. Dense thickets provide sanctuary from the enemy above.

Jungle cats will still accept an angler's offerings but only on their terms. To be successful, you

When cats are ambushing prey from the thick cover of weed beds and dense timber, the angler may have to use pinpoint fishing tactics to capture his quarry.

must be willing to make a slow, cautious, difficult entry into the flooded jungle.

Jungle Hideouts
Not every patch of thick cover will hold big cats. The best provide easy movement between shallow and deep water. Look for brushpiles, fallen trees, inundated willows and buckbrush, flooded timber, and other dense woody cover along channel drop-offs, underwater humps and holes, the edges of shallow flats, and other fast-breaking structures. Other "jungle" hideouts hold big cats, too, but these are among the best.

One hotspot to investigate is where several trees have washed out and toppled into the water on an outside stream bend. Outside bends usually have deep pockets of water adjacent to a channel break. Add the thick cover provided by branchy underwater treetops, and you have an ideal jungle cat hideout.

Jungle Gear
Heavy line and tackle are a must for this type of fishing. Use at least twenty- to twenty-five-pound-test line and a long stout rod. Strong

line is a necessity when hossing big battlewise cats out of these hideaways. You don't want to let a hooked fish fiddle around in the cover. Get it out of there if you can, and let it do its fighting closer to the boat or shore. The long rod gives you a fighting advantage and allows you to better fish dense thickets where casting is virtually impossible.

If you're fishing from a boat, take along a big landing net, too. It's tough getting a giant catfish in a boat under any circumstances, but the right-sized net can help tame your quarry.

Another tip: set your drag just barely below your line's breaking point. You don't want a big brushpile cat peeling off any more line than necessary, or you'll be hung up in an instant.

Jungle Warfare
Now that you're properly armed and on the field of combat, you need to plan the logistics of your attack. Fact is, there's only one way to

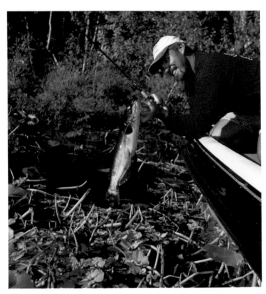

Catfish often bury themselves in thick cover. The angler must move in close and fish his rig in small openings to find success.

go about it: you have to get right in there with them for close-quarters combat.

With a bobber rig, there's less chance of getting snagged beneath the surface. A slip bobber is best because it allows you to reel your entire rig right up to the rod tip. This allows more freedom to work the rig back into cover.

Any standard catfish bait can be used, but for jungle cats, cut shad or carp are hard to beat. Big cats love cutbait, and it won't tangle itself up like live minnows or crawfish. Thread a chunk about two inches square on a 3/0 hook, and unless the current is strong, don't use any weight.

Get within rod's reach of the cover and work slowly and precisely, moving your rig over, under, through, or around the cover until you can ease it down in an opening. You may catch a few nice cats along the edge of the cover but most will be buried in it, striking only when you put the bait right on their nose.

When you do get a strike, react immediately, setting the hook hard and reeling like crazy. You must get a good hookset and pull the fish out of cover before it has time to tie you up. That's why heavy tackle is so important. This battle requires brawn not finesse.

Fishing for jungle cats can be extremely frustrating. You get hung up a lot trying to move your rig into an open pocket. You get hung up when you're in the pocket. Then, if by some miracle you haven't hung yourself up, the cat will do it for you. Only after considerable practice will you overcome these obstacles to your sanity.

The nice thing is, practice makes perfect. And if you stick with it long enough, odds are you'll eventually land one of the biggest catfish you've ever laid eyes on. The safari may exhaust you physically and mentally, but when that fat jungle cat is finally flouncing in the bottom of your boat, you'll know it was worth the extra effort.

Catfish on the Rocks

Rock-covered shores attract catfish searching for meals and spawning sites.

My dictionary defines riprap as "a wall or foundation of broken stones thrown together irregularly." I'd have to go a step further and describe riprap as among the most outstanding yet often overlooked places to catch catfish in a river or lake.

Few other types of shoreline cover hold large numbers of catfish as consistently as does riprap. Put a dozen men on a strange lake and let them all fish different types of structures for one day, and for numbers of fish caught, I'll bet on the guy who picked the riprap. This type of shoreline cover holds catfish year-round.

argeting the riprapped bank in the background roduced this nice Mississippi River blue cat for)klahoma catfish angler Jeff Williams.

Riprap is a covering of rocks used to reduce shoreline erosion. It provides cover, depth, shade, protection, and food—everything a catfish could desire—making a top fishing area wherever it is found.

Riprap is found on nearly every lake and on many rivers, and when you stop to think about it, you can see why this type of rocky structure is appealing to catfish. One reason is because riprap provides a home for Mr. Whiskers' primary food supplies. Algae grow on the submerged stones. Shad and minnows are attracted to the vegetation. Catfish arrive to eat the baitfish.

Every ten-year-old boy knows that crayfish—a favored forage of cats—thrive under rocks, often in the form of riprap bordering lakes and streams. These rock walls are often the only decent crayfish habitat in an entire lake, and catfish will stack up to feed on these tasty morsels. I've taken cats on riprap with as many as two dozen crayfish in their stomachs.

Another reason riprap provides good catfishing is because the rocks provide good basic habitat structure. There is cover, depth, shade, and protection. Riprap is usually found near deep water since it's most often found around bridges, causeways, or roadways that cross channels or near the dam itself.

Another major plus is that riprap is extensive. Even if you fail to find fish concentrated on a certain spot, you can often cover enough riprap on a river or lake to take home a limit.

Riprap plays a strong role in big-river catfishing simply because there is typically so much of it along the river channel. On the Arkansas River in Arkansas, for instance, there are hundreds of long rock walls known as wing dikes. The US Army Corps of Engineers placed these in strategic locations up and down the McClellan-Kerr Navigation System to help direct water into the main river channel to prevent erosion.

The wing dikes have functioned as they were intended and have also proved to be a boon to the area's summer catfishermen. During June, July, and August, as water temperatures soar, channel, blue, and flathead catfish concentrate along the riprap where there is slight current. Anglers may occasionally take a large trophy catfish along river riprap, but most of these fish weigh ten pounds or fewer.

Tips for Riprap Catfishing

When fishing river riprap for catfish, the first place to begin your search for fish is along the very ends of the rocks. If the catfish aren't there, gradually work your way past other areas along the riprap. Sometimes an unusual feature along the wing dikes will attract and hold a school of catfish.

If you're fishing a long wing dike that is uniform in appearance, look it over, up, and down, keying in on objects or contour changes that distinguish a small section of the wall from its surroundings. Sometimes a tree washed in will be enough to attract catfish. Other times a difference in the rocks will do the trick. Look for spots where big boulders change to smaller rocks. Points, cuts, pipes, and culverts all create something different and may attract catfish.

At the same time you're checking the riprap for these peculiarities, you should check for unusual bottom features with a sonar unit. The alert angler will check closely for a creek

The author's son, Matt Sutton, brings in a nice channel cat caught on a long stretch of riprapped bank on the Missouri River. The cats were concentrated near the big rock on which Matt stands, one of the few variable structures on an otherwise lookalike stretch of shore.

channel that borders a wall, submerged humps, a pit, some brush, a submerged roadbed used during the riprap's construction, or some other nuance that might tend to concentrate fish on a structure that may extend for miles.

The rules about fishing the ends of the rocks first and locating unusual features also hold true for riprap on lakes for the same general reasons. Currents and wind-pushed waves washing over the end of a riprap dike create an eddy or calm water zone around the back side of those rocks and at the same time carry food downstream. This is not the case where waves wash straight into the riprap.

While cats don't necessarily hold in this slack-water eddy, they may swim in and out of it, moving over the end of the rocks in the process. Of course, this all depends on current flows and wave force, as well as on the movements of prey items, such as shad. If you've ever observed a school of shad or other baitfish swimming along the rocks, you know they stay in schools that are forever moving. They move up and down the rock walls and around the ends, and catfish often follow.

Bridge riprap can be especially important in lakes. Bridges usually span creeks, rivers, or connecting channels, and the bridge area often represents the deepest water in the area. Fish concentrate near distinctive features such as bridges. This happens as fish are funneled into the narrow section of water where a bridge crosses a lake or reservoir. Also movement between two areas separated by a bridge is restricted to this relatively confined area. Some moving catfish are going to make this area their home or at least remain long enough to feed in the shallows before continuing on. Food is carried through these man-made funnels by current. Catfish take advantage of this and hold out of the flow on the downstream side to check out the selection of groceries washing past.

When fishing bridge riprap, the four corners formed as the riprap bank gives way to the bridge superstructure are always worth a few casts regardless of the presence of other structures. These corners form semi-points that often hold several catfish. The downcurrent points are best, as these are ideal ambush spots for catfish. Cast into the current from a boat stationed on the bridge's downcurrent or downwind side. This allows your bait to move downcurrent in a natural manner.

Under tough windy or post-frontal conditions, bridge riprap may produce catfish when fishing other areas proves fruitless. The feeding habits of bridge-oriented cats seem to be less affected by these conditions than do those of other catfish populations.

During windy weather, bridge riprap excels due to the funnel effect discussed earlier. Wind increases the flow of water and food through the area. Resident catfish react instinctively to the wind and line up to feed on baitfish blown into the rock walls. Also, as the wind throws choppy water on the rocky bank, crayfish are stirred up and become easy pickings for feeding cats. Unless there are safety risks, the riprap angler welcomes a good wind, and so do catfish, especially during hot summer months.

Because bridge-oriented catfish are primarily deep-water residents that move occasionally into the food-filled shallows, weather fronts tend to have less of an adverse effect on them. If the creek or river channel beneath the bridge is fairly deep, catfish can avoid much of the trauma associated with a strong front. Catfish also find shade from harsh post-frontal sunlight around bridge pilings and beneath the superstructure itself. Often by fishing bridge riprap, a catfish angler can avoid most of the post-front doldrums. In any case, bridges and the associated riprap are usually good for a catfish or two under normally adverse conditions.

The Angling Approach

Although catfish fans can and do fish riprap areas from the bank with much success, riprap fishing from a boat allows one to present the bait in a more natural manner. This also enables the angler to work much greater expanses of riprap than would be possible on foot from the shore.

ne reason riprap attracts catfish is because it also racts favored food animals, such as crayfish.

Where's the best place to catfish on a long stretch of lookalike riprap? Look for points in the rocks, areas where big rocks change to smaller rocks, woody cover adjacent the riprap, or anything else that is different from the norm.

The fisherman should position his boat downstream below the end of the rocks and cast upstream. Use only enough weight to keep the bait moving slowly just over the bottom, and allow the bait to come down with the current, following the same natural movement of real food.

Allow the bait to settle near the end of the rocks on some casts and in the eddy zone behind the rocks on others. And if the normal downstream retrieve doesn't produce a fish, cast downcurrent and try retrieving upstream. Just because you don't hook a cat on the downstream retrieve doesn't mean the fish aren't there. Work the rocks carefully to find the best pattern before moving somewhere else.

After working the end of the wing dikes, try making long casts parallel to the rocks, fishing different depths. During the day, catfish will generally hold in deeper water; at night they'll move into the shallows to feed. When the current has swung your line to the end of its arc and it's remaining tight and stationary, allow the bait to stay there for several minutes. Catfish are drawn to food by taste and scent, and moving the bait too soon can lessen your chances of catching fish.

Baits for Riprap

There are as many different baits for catfish as there are catfishermen to use them. Every cat man has his favorite, but some work better than others when fishing riprap.

As mentioned earlier, baitfish and crayfish are at home in this rocky environment, so naturally shad, minnows, and crayfish are the basic bait choices. A three-way rig with the weight and hook on separate lines will save a lot of rerigging. The weights often fall in crevices between rocks, lodging and causing a hang-up. Rig a weight line that's of lesser breaking

Catalpa worms, the larvae of the catalpa sphinx moth, are often gathered from catalpa trees and used by catfishermen targeting riprap catfish.

strength than your main line and hook line, and all you'll lose to a hang-up is your lead.

Some riprap catfishermen use catalpa worms for bait. They're easy to acquire, attractive to catfish, and stay on the hook even in swift water. Night crawlers are always good baits, but when stream fishing, you're apt to catch more drum on them than catfish. Doughbaits don't usually hold to the hook well in current, but sponge baits and dip baits are fantastic for all types of riprap catfishing.

If you're fishing specifically for flatheads, live bait is the only way to go. Small bream, goldfish, or minnows hooked through the lips or behind the dorsal fin can bring smashing strikes. Blue cats seem to prefer cut or whole shad.

Don't overlook artificials for catching catfish. There are many baitfish- and crawfish-imitating crankbaits that will take cats when bounced through the rocks. Deep-diving models work better, as the longer bill helps keep the line from snagging. Riprap catfish also will hit a variety of jigs and spinners.

Riprap offers all the things catfish need for living high on the hog, so it's little wonder you find so many catfish on the rocks. What is surprising is the number of catfish anglers who overlook riprap as a source of great catfishing. If you're one of those anglers who continues to cruise right past this great structure, stop next time and take a second look at those rocky riprap walls. They may save you a lot of otherwise fishless days.

Cure Bad Habits for Trophy Cats

The catfish may not have lockjaw. It could be the error of your ways that is preventing you from catching them.

"What can I do to catch more trophy catfish?"

Many anglers want a simple answer to that question, but unfortunately, there's rarely one to be found. I've been chasing catfish for decades and have learned that no magic formula ensures success every time we fish for big blues, flatheads, and channel cats.

One thing is certain, though; when we're having an unproductive fishing day, as often as not it's due to our own errors—not because trophy catfish are exceptionally evasive or tight-lipped.

The cure? Do some self-analysis and determine if you're missing fish because of bad habits. This chapter will help you do that.

Bad habit #1: Using the wrong bait.
Remember that kid Mikey in the old Life cereal commercials? His friends try the new breakfast food on this freckle-faced youngster because they say, "He'll eat anything."

Many anglers think catfish are like Mikey. They believe no matter what food is on the table or river bottom, catfish will eat it. In fact, many folks believe catfish behave like underwater vultures, cleaning lake and river bottoms of carrion and garbage. Consequently, they say, it matters not what type of bait you use for catfish, and indeed, the more rotten and smelly the bait, the more likely a big catfish will find and eat it.

To some extent, they're right. Catfish are scavengers and aren't really picky about their food. But this applies primarily to small catfish.

For example, I've caught thousands of channel and blue cats on homemade and commercial stinkbaits. But fish caught using prepared baits are usually fewer than five pounds. Trophy specimens are rarely enticed with our favorite stinkbaits.

Consider flatheads, as well. Small ones will hit prepared baits, crawfish, worms, and other enticements without hesitation. If it's heavyweights you're seeking, however, these baits don't work so well. A meat and potatoes meal for a giant flathead is another fish—a live fish—such as a

Anglers must use the right baits when targeting trophy catfish, or their efforts will fail. For example, a live herring such as this is an ideal bait for a trophy flathead, but dead baits, grocery baits, and commercial baits rarely entice heavyweights of this species.

The author yanked this nice flathead from its hiding place in dense cover using a live fish bait. Targeting each species of catfish in the right place using the right bait is key to the angler's success.

bullhead, chub, sucker, or sunfish. Trophy flatheads rarely eat anything except live fish.

The bottom line is this, and scientific studies have shown it to be so: a catfish twenty-four inches or longer, regardless of species, sustains itself on a diet comprised almost exclusively of other fish. For flatheads, this means live fish. Trophy blues and channel cats will devour dead baits, too, but even so, the best dead baits are fresh baits. A chunk of rotten, smelly shad or herring won't work nearly as well as a chunk cut from a just-caught baitfish.

Remember these things when fishing. If you want to catch lots of catfish up to twenty-four inches long, almost any bait from chicken liver to worms will work. But if it's trophies you're after, you'll improve your chance of hooking up if you use fresh or live fish baits.

Bad habit #2: Failure to use tactics specific to species and locale.

A catfish is a catfish is a catfish, right? This is another way of saying all catfish are alike, and

tactics that work for one species work for all. Many anglers fish as if this were so, but it is not.

Each catfish species exhibits behaviors specific to that species. Consequently, we must gear our tactics toward the particular species we hope to catch to enjoy success.

For example, trophy blue cats behave much like striped bass. They feed primarily on shad, herring, and other schooling highly mobile baitfish. Consequently, big blues are more migratory than other cats and more frequently found in open-water habitats.

While big blues and channel cats often congregate in loose schools containing several trophy-class individuals, flatheads are more solitary fish. Rarely will you catch more than one trophy flathead in a single fishing hole. Flatheads are cover lovers, as well, hiding in brush, log piles, and cavities to ambush prey. Channel cats and blues sometimes do this, too, but not as frequently as their big brown cousins.

Flatheads almost always are caught in or near some type of dense cover, while blues and channel cats most often are not.

These are just two examples showing species behavior differences. Space does not permit an in-depth dissertation here. Yet knowing just these things, we can immediately improve our odds for success.

For example, let's say we're fishing a reservoir bristling with sizeable flatheads but few blue cats. If we fish offshore structures, such as river channels and humps—a productive means for busting big blues—we might fish years without catching a trophy catfish because the more abundant flatheads rarely if ever use these habitats. If we focused our efforts on nearshore cover, such as laydowns and drift piles, however, we might quickly find success—if we use live baits—because big flatheads love these spots.

To use another example, let's say we're fishing a big river with healthy populations of all three major catfish species. If the only bait we have is cutbait, and we spend our time fishing near dense shoreline cover, we reduce our chances of catching a trophy fish because flatheads, which prefer live bait, are the predominant species here. If we move offshore, however, and use our fish-finder to locate big fish holding near shad schools around bottom structures, our success rate should improve because this is the realm of trophy-class blues and channel cats, which love cutbait.

The concept I'm trying to get across is simple, really. We must target the predominant species of catfish in each body of water using tactics specific to that species. And to do this, we must learn the specific behavior patterns exhibited by big blue, channel, and flathead catfish. Failure to do so will lead to frustration because trophy cats will be caught by chance and not by design. And when we leave things up to

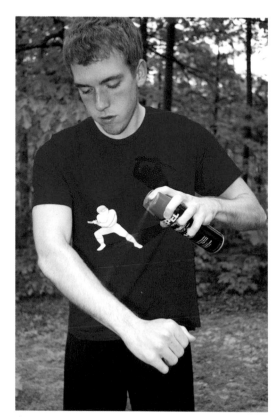

Anglers should never lose sight of the fact that catfish are easily repelled by things such as insect repellent, gasoline, tobacco, and sunscreen. If even a minute quantity touches the bait, a catfish won't bite.

chance, the odds for success rarely fall in our favor.

Bad habit #3: Ignoring the catfish's extraordinary sensory abilities.

This bad habit is one of the most prevalent, yet few anglers realize an inability to catch trophy catfish may be caused by something as commonplace as applying sunscreen or casting a shadow across our fishing hole. Let me explain.

Catfish have turbo-charged senses. Take taste, for example. When it comes to this sense, no creature on earth can compare. A catfish has dense concentrations of taste buds all over its body and not just in the mouth. The densest concentrations are on the gill rakers, so the fish can taste things in the water flowing over the gills. But taste buds cover the outside of the catfish, as well—whiskers, fins, back, belly, sides, and even the tail.

The catfish's olfactory sense is amazingly keen, as well. Without going into a lot of anatomical details, let's just say they can smell some compounds at the incredibly low concentration of one part per ten billion parts of water. That's how acute this sense is. And the sense of taste has a comparable level of acuteness.

These powerful senses enable catfish to thrive in turbid water and various areas where other fish cannot. A catfish can zero in on food even without the benefit of sight, using only the senses of smell and taste.

These sensory abilities also benefit anglers because they help catfish find the angler's bait even in adverse conditions.

What many people don't consider is the fact that catfish also can easily detect things in the water they don't like, and these compounds can be tasted and smelled by catfish even in extremely minute quantities. According to scientists who've studied catfish senses, such turn-offs include gasoline and ingredients found in commonly used products, such as sunscreen, tobacco, and insect repellent. It stands to reason, then, if you apply sunscreen or insect repellent with your hands or accidentally get gas on yourself and later handle bait with your hands, you may be repelling the catfish you're hoping to catch. Your catch rate will improve if you avoid contact with such materials as much as possible.

Other senses can work against anglers, as well. For example, catfish have very good eyesight despite popular misconceptions. And while they do not rely on this sense as much in waters where visibility is limited, it plays a key role in their behavior in waters that are clear.

Did you know, for instance, that catfish will spook when a shadow crosses the water? Biologists learned this while conducting lab experiments that could be fouled up for weeks simply because someone put their hand over the top of an aquarium. This may be of no concern to a catfish angler fishing muddy water because fish in muddy water don't see shadows from above. When fishing clear water, however, you'll rarely catch a cat while fishing beneath your boat or in water upon which you're casting a shadow. That's one reason many catfishermen are more successful at night—no shadows. And it's a good reason to always keep the sun in your face or to your side, not at your back, to avoid casting a shadow on the water you're fishing.

Here's another fact you may not have known. The lateral line and advanced hearing system of a catfish help it detect low-frequency sound vibrations. Creatures scurrying across the bottom, flopping at the surface, swimming through the water, or walking along shore all create low-frequency vibrations catfish can sense. This "vibrational" sense is so keen, some cultures have used catfish for centuries to warn of earthquakes.

This is not a problem for savvy anglers who fish with a measure of stealth. But go stomping along the shore, and you can spook catfish—including big catfish—even when you're many yards away. And the sound of a dropped paddle or sinker is like a warning siren to your quarry.

Knowing these things, you can see why it's very important to be aware of the catfish's extraordinary sensory abilities at all times. If you don't, your catch rate will fall.

Bad habit #4: Fishing only on the bottom.
Catfish are well-adapted for feeding on the bottom of rivers, lakes, and ponds, but if you think they never feed at mid-depths or on the surface, you're wrong. Trophy blue and channel cats often suspend at mid-depths to prey on baitfish, such as shad and herring. And at times when frogs are plentiful, for example, big cats will come to the surface to gobble up their dinner. Working a live frog topside is one of the best of all ways to catch a channel cat weighing more than twenty pounds.

If bottom fishing doesn't produce a bite within a reasonable time, watch for surface activity—particularly in summer and near dawn or dusk—that indicates fish are taking their food at the surface, or watch your sonar for suspended fish and use a float rig to present bait at the proper level.

Bad habit #5: Fishing only during summer.
For some reason, many people associate catfishing with summer. In fact, many aficionados restrict their fishing to this season alone. There's nothing wrong with this; lots of trophy cats are caught by anglers during hot weather. Summer, however, is not necessarily the best season for catching heavyweight whiskerfish. Anglers who learn to find and pattern catfish during other seasons often discover the bite is even better when the water and the weather are cooler.

Those who regularly catch trophy blue cats often do so by fishing deep ledges in winter. Normally sedentary flatheads roam and feed ravenously during high water in spring and again in autumn prior to entering a period of winter torpor. Channel cats bite spring, summer, fall, and winter. Ice fishermen often catch them.

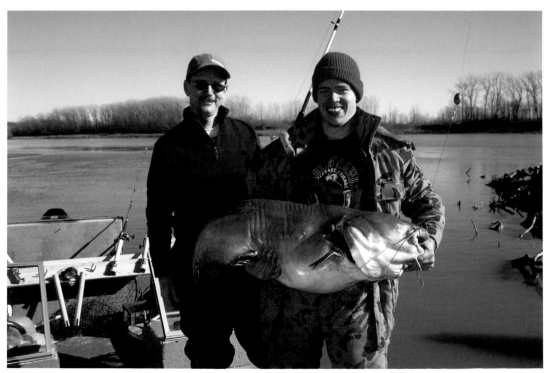

Many anglers associate catfishing with the hot summer months, but other seasons may be more productive for trophy cats such as this big winter blue.

The worst time to fish? During the spawn, which usually peaks in early summer. Egg-laying females and nest-guarding males are in cavities and may not feed at all for a period of days or weeks.

Conclusion

At times, nothing we do can entice a trophy catfish to bite. For reasons we don't fully understand, big fish often become inactive and darn near impossible to catch.

It's important to remember, though, that a poor catch rate may be totally unrelated to the level of catfish activity. Frequently, it's just a result of our own bad habits. To increase the odds of hooking a beefy blue, channel cat, or flathead, examine your tactics now and then, and be sure you're doing everything correctly to the best of your ability. Getting rid of bad habits may be the best way of all to ensure success when you hope to catch a trophy.

More Bad Habits

Using dull hooks buried in bait. Many cat fans don't have problems finding fish, yet they're continually frustrated when they can't hook those that bite. To cure this problem, always fish with sharp, exposed hooks. Run the hook point over a fingernail. Sharp hooks dig in. Those that skate across the nail without catching should be honed or replaced. And instead of burying your hook in bait, leave the barb exposed. Catfish won't notice. More hookups will result.

Using the wrong rig. It's important to learn a variety of rigs and use each when appropriate. A simple egg-sinker rig may work great in a pond but not a river. Drift rigs may be needed when cats are scattered and hard to find. A specialty rig, such as the float-paternoster, is best when fishing large live baits. Learn more rigs, catch more cats.

No sonar. A sonar fish-finder helps pinpoint big catfish on structures and cover you'd otherwise miss. Buy one, learn to use it, and use it often.

Fishing the wrong waters. Trophy catfish seldom come from creeks, ponds, and small lakes. It happens occasionally but not enough to merit your attention. When seeking a true heavyweight, focus your fishing efforts on large rivers and lakes.

Lack of persistence. Persistence is one of the most important qualities of those who frequently catch trophy catfish. Anyone can learn the tactics necessary for catching cats, but to catch trophy fish, you must keep bait in the water where the big ones swim. Learn everything you can about a lake or river where you know those big fish are. Then stay at it, day after day after day, learning more. Catfishermen who do that have the best chance of catching the catfish of a lifetime.

Alternative Tactics

Jug Fishing

You'll be hard-pressed to find a form of catfishing more fun than jug fishing.

"Thar she blows!"

When a big catfish pulls a jug under, the call rings out. The fish isn't as big as Moby Dick, of course, but this is as close to whaling as you can get in a river or lake.

My fishing buddy paddles hurriedly, trying to pull our johnboat alongside the speeding milk jug. The catfish pulling the jug wants no part of this. The jug sounds and then reappears twenty feet away.

My friend moves fast. This time, we reach the jug before it submerges. I swing a big landing net beneath it and bring up a ten-pound channel cat, our third of the afternoon. Before it's unhooked, another jug cuts a wake across the river.

"Thar she blows again!"

For pure country boy fun, nothing equals jug fishing for cats. Decades ago, folks called it "blocking" because blocks of wood were used to float the participants' catfishing rigs. Nowadays, empty milk or soda jugs are more likely to be used. Save a few, tie on some line, add hooks, bait 'em up, and you're ready to jug fish. The only other necessities are a boat, a paddle or trolling motor for pursuing your

Jug fishing is a simple, old-fashioned method of catfishing that can provide long hours of fun and excitement.

quarry, and a big net for landing the cats you hook. You can fish with jugs in any body of water where catfish live from small ponds to big rivers and lakes.

Making Jug Rigs

Any narrow-necked plastic container with a tight-fitting lid can be used. I prefer one- to two-liter soda bottles. When sprayed with fluorescent orange, chartreuse, or black paint, they're easy to see, and most catfish can't hold one under too long. The latter characteristic is important because you want the jug to exhaust the catfish enough that you can more easily net the fish.

I rig each jug with soft Dacron or braided line because it doesn't get as loopy and hard to handle as monofilament. Use fifty-pound-test or more in case you hook a whopper. Tie directly to the jug's handle or neck if you like, but jugs tip up better, signaling strikes, if you attach line to the cap instead. Do this by drilling a small hole through the cap, running the line through the cap from outside to in, and tying to a small metal washer on the inside so the line won't pull back through. Screw the cap back on, and you're ready.

Tie plenty of line to each jug, then lengthen or shorten it as needed. Do this by wrapping line around the jug and securing it with tape or a rubber band or by loosening the washer and stuffing line inside the jug. The latter method is best if you want the jugs to tip up when a cat takes the bait.

For cats up to fifteen pounds, I use one or two 1/0 to 3/0 circle hooks, which usually impale the fish in the corner of the mouth. Two hooks rigged tandem, one above the other, allow you to test different depths. When trophy cats are targeted, I prefer 5/0 or larger circle hooks that

A coating of brightly colored paint improves the visibility of jugs used for floats.

accommodate larger baits. Each hook must be needle sharp.

It's sometimes helpful to tie a bell sinker above or below each hook to hold the bait near bottom and to slow movement of the jugs when it's windy. Add your favorite bait—fish pieces, night crawlers, hot dogs, stinkbait chunks, etc.—then release the jugs several feet apart and let them drift in the breeze or current. Check regulations for jug fishing restrictions before you go, and limit the number of jugs you use so you can properly watch them and be sure none are lost and left to litter the lake or river.

Float your rigs near catfish-attracting structures and cover for more hookups, but always fish several feet away from tree tops and rocks so your jugs won't snag. Follow at a distance so you don't spook fish, but be ready to react the moment you see action.

Ready for Action

Each jug functions like a big fishing bobber. When a catfish bites, the jug stops and bobs. When the bait is swallowed, one of two things happens—the jug zips away across the water or it disappears beneath the surface. This is where the fun really starts.

Move in as fast as you can and try to grab the jug, dip a landing net beneath it, or snag the line with a long pole that has a hook on the end. When using your hands, grab the jug but never the line. If you grab the line, you could get tangled or cut. If you've hooked a small catfish, you probably won't have much trouble. But when a big cat takes the bait, the jug may sound then pop up several yards away time and time again before you get close enough to snare the rig. Spooked catfish may surge away every time you get near. For this reason, it's best to take a buddy each time you go jug fishing. One of you paddles or operates the motor during the pursuit. The other stands ready to capture the fleeing cat. Both wear life jackets, in case of an unexpected spill.

Fishing with Pool Noodles

A modernized method of jug fishing employs floats made from the long, hollow, closed-foam noodles that kids float on in swimming pools. These signal a strike better than regular jugs because when a fish takes your bait, the noodle stands up and waves around.

Cut one five-foot noodle into three twenty-inch floats. Drill a hole through each noodle from one side to the other about four inches from one end. Make the hole large enough to accommodate a piece of plastic drinking straw or metal tubing as long as the noodle is wide. Run the straw or tubing through the hole. This serves as a protective sleeve that keeps your fishing line from cutting through the foam when a fish is on.

Next, cut a four-foot piece of stout fishing line. Run it through the sleeve, and tie the line securely around the noodle. To the line's lower end, tie a three-way swivel. To the swivel's bottom eye, tie another piece of line six feet long. Add a hook and sinker to this. To the other eye of the swivel, tie a two-foot leader line with a hook on the end. Rigged this way, you can fish two baits at different depths, which should increase your catch.

If you're "noodling" at night, add reflective tape around each noodle's top so it shines when a flashlight beam hits it.

When the noodles aren't in use, just wrap the line around each one and plant the barbs of the

Empty plastic bottles aren't the only floats used for jug fishing. Many anglers now use foam pool noodles to make highly effective and inexpensive rigs.

Pool noodle floats can be stored in a milk crate or box until use.

hooks in the foam to keep everything in place. You can place a dozen or more in a plastic crate or big garbage bag for carrying. Then when you get to the lake or river, all you have to do is unroll the lines, bait the hooks, and drop the noodle rigs in the water.

Good baits include night crawlers, minnows, chunk-style commercial baits, and pieces of hot dogs.

Jug fishing is a simple way to catch catfish, tailor-made for children and adults who never grew up. Load up this season and give it a try. For high-level excitement and downright fun, nothing beats jug fishing.

Yo-yo Fishing

For some fast-paced catfishing fun, try this specialized form of limblining.

Billy "Toothpick" Blakley reminded me how much fun playing with yo-yos can be.

We were supposed to be catching the giant bluegills inhabiting Tennessee's Reelfoot Lake. Unfortunately, the bluegills played hard to get. After a long almost-fishless morning, I suggested to Toothpick, who is a fishing guide at Blue Bank Resort, that we do something different.

"How 'bout yo-yos?" he inquired.

"What?" I asked.

"Yo-yos," he said. "Let's go yo-yoing."

Don't misunderstand. Toothpick wasn't talking about walking the dog or doing a sleeper with my Duncan yo-yo. In the South, if a grown man asks you to go yo-yoing, he's not asking you to play with a kid's toy. In this region, adults probably yo-yo a lot more than kids nowadays. The difference is, the kids are playing and the adults are fishing, although there are those who maintain the two are one and the same.

White's Auto-Fisher

In fishing parlance, yo-yo is a nickname for the Automatic Fishing Reel, or Auto-Fisher, a neat little mechanical device patented on July 12, 1949 by John W. White Jr., a native of Arkansas. White had the notion that if a fisherman can

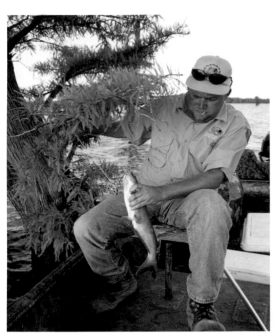

Billy "Toothpick" Blakley brings in a nice channel cat taken on a yo-yo in Tennessee's Reelfoot Lake. The low-hanging branches of cypress trees make ideal anchor points for these automatic fishing devices.

use ten times as many hooks, chances are he can catch ten times as many fish. Multihook trot-lines weren't to his liking because they are too restrictive. He preferred to pick several individual hotspots and fish all of them at once, so using individual fishing units was the only answer.

White's original prototype incorporated the spring-loaded end of an old window shade. It consisted of a carbon-steel spring, a galvanized steel reel, a ratchet, and a body to hold it all together. Interestingly, the only important change over the years came when White began painting Auto-Fishers fluorescent orange so they could be spotted more easily at a distance.

The Auto-Fisher's "yo-yo" nickname makes sense when you see one in action. A length of nylon line is stored on the spring-loaded reel.

The line runs through a metal ear with a hole in it, and a snap swivel and hook are placed on the line's end. If you pull on the line's end, the reel turns, and line comes out. If you release the line, it snaps back, rewound on the spool by the action of the spring. The line stops rewinding when the swivel becomes seated against the metal ear.

Placing and Setting Yo-yos

Yo-yos usually are hung singly from tree limbs, docks, poles, or other stable objects above the water. The hook is baited first, then line is pulled off the retractable spool, and a catch, or trigger, is set in a notch on the spool to hold the line at the preferred depth. When a fish takes the bait, the catch is released, and the spring tension pulls the line tight. This sets the hook in the fish's mouth. The fish is then fighting the spring, and it is eventually worn down. The

The line on a yo-yo can be lengthened or shortened to suit various fishing situations.

spring tension can be set at hard, medium, or light. The yo-yoer comes around periodically to remove his catch and reset the lines.

With the help of two friends, Toothpick and I set out seventy-five yo-yos. Reelfoot Lake provides an ideal setting for yo-yo fishing thanks to the abundance of cypress trees growing out in the lake. Each cypress has low-hanging branches where the yo-yos can be attached, and because the trees grow in clusters, you can set dozens of yo-yos where they all can be watched.

Yo-yo Baits
Toothpick prefers night crawlers or other earthworms above other baits.

"Small channel cats are abundant in Reelfoot," he told me. "And experience has shown me that worms are as good a bait as any when you're after small cats for the dinner table. You can buy a couple of hundred worms at any bait store for a pretty reasonable price, and that's plenty when you're fishing a few dozen yo-yos."

Select your bait based on the type of catfish you want to catch. Worms are excellent for small channel cats, but equally productive baits include chicken liver, catalpa worms, crawfish, stink-baits, and minnows. Live fish baits—minnows, goldfish, small sunfish, etc.—are best for flat-heads. Blue cats fall for cut shad or herring.

Toothpick and I tied each yo-yo to a branch near the water, baited the hook, then stripped off enough line to keep the baits four feet or so beneath the water. Although the swivels at each line's end were ample to weight the baits we used, some yo-yo fishermen add big split shot or other weights to keep their baits down, particularly when fishing areas with current.

In the cypress groves we fished, baits placed nearest to each tree's trunk produced best. Ini-tially, some yo-yos were placed near the trunk, others at the ends of branches several feet away from the trunk. When we determined that in-close yo-yos were producing more cats, we moved the outer devices closer to the trunks.

Proper Placement and Tracking
"Just because you have a lot of hooks in the water doesn't mean you're going to catch a lot of catfish," Toothpick said. "It's important to place each hook in a spot where catfish are likely to be feeding. Experimenting with different presentations can help you determine the best spots on a particular day, but it's important to learn the specific types of cover and structure catfish prefer in order to be a successful yo-yo fisherman time and time again. If you place your rigs in fishless water, you won't catch fish, simple as that."

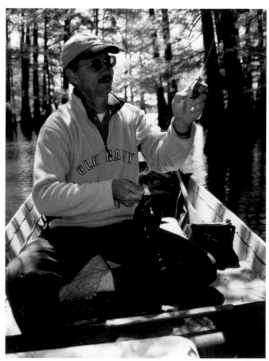

Fishing with yo-yos allows the angler to choose several prime fishing locales and fish them all at once.

At times, you may be able to place and set all your yo-yos before the catfish start biting. But at other times, you'll be setting one out when you hear a catfish fighting the line on another one you already baited. Toothpick and I experienced the latter. Before we had placed all seventy-five of our yo-yos, we had already caught ten nice channel cats.

"It's important to monitor your yo-yos closely in order to avoid exceeding the creel limit," Toothpick says. And always practice selective harvest. Keep smaller cats for eating, and release the big guys to maintain the trophy stock.

The popularity of yo-yos is easy to understand. Many fishermen use them to stock their freezers for the winter at times when the fishing is at its best. Lots of fish can be taken quickly with yo-yos, and sometimes, time is of the essence. Using yo-yos is a good way to gather the makings for a fish fry, especially when only one man is responsible for obtaining the supply.

Fishing with yo-yos is pure unadulterated fun. You can't "walk the dog" with a White's Auto-Fisher, but you can "catch the cat." Try it and see.

Yo-yoing the Right Way

Yo-yos are illegal in some states. In other states, there are numerous restrictions on yo-yo fishing. In my home state of Arkansas, for example, it is illegal to suspend more than one yo-yo from any horizontal line, wire, limb, or support. It also is unlawful to leave yo-yos unattended (out of sight or hearing), except from sunset to sunrise when each yo-yo is clearly marked with the name and address of the user.

Always know your local regulations and abide by them.

There is an effort underway by some irate anglers to have yo-yos banned altogether. This is largely due to a small group of slob fishermen who don't properly attend their yo-yos. An unattended yo-yo can be a hazard to fishermen, and if left unchecked, many fish are hooked and die, a lamentable waste. Yo-yo fishermen can help eliminate the opposition to this enjoyable sport by following regulations, removing their catch as soon as possible, and removing all yo-yos following every outing.

Keeping Track

Keeping track of all the yo-yos you have out is important. Common sense requires it because you don't want to leave a yo-yo unattended where your catch will die and spoil. In some states, the law requires you to set all your yo-yos in a small area so they can be watched constantly.

When I fish with yo-yos, I track those I have out by several methods. First, I try to set all my yo-yos along a straight line course—along a river bank, along the edge of a tree line, etc. That way I don't have to look all over the place for my sets. I follow a straight line from one end of my sets to the other then back again. Each yo-yo is placed in sight of the one before it. And each time I run my yo-yo line, I count the devices to be sure none have been missed.

A splotch of fluorescent paint sprayed on each yo-yo helps immensely when you're trying to spot them, or you can tie a small piece of flagging tape to the end of each branch on which a yo-yo is suspended. When I'm finished fishing, I count my yo-yos again to be sure none are missing. I never leave a yo-yo behind and neither should you.

Yo-yo Tips

- Most successful yo-yoers agree conditions are best in spring when ravenous catfish are more likely to be roaming the shallows.

- Green timber flooded by spring overflows is an especially productive place to fish with yo-yos.

- When fishing waters with few overhanging limbs, carry a hammer and some sixteen-penny nails. Drive nails into stumps and logs—never into live trees—and hang your yo-yos there. Remove the nails when you leave.

- Try tying a yo-yo beneath each jug when jug fishing. You'll get a higher percentage of hook sets, but you'll have to use two-liter jugs or bigger.

- Some yo-yo fishermen prefer lively fish, frogs, or salamanders rigged on short lines so they wiggle and thrash right at the water's surface. Tie to your anchor point, then pull out enough line to keep the baited hook just below the top of the water. This is a deadly setup for attracting hungry catfish.

- When rigged with appropriately sized hooks and baits, yo-yos can be used to catch crappie, bluegills, and other sportfish in addition to catfish. Check local regulations for restrictions.

Make Your Own Trotline

Trotlining is more exciting than you think. Don't knock it till you've tried it.

"I don't understand why anyone would want to trotline for catfish," a friend says. "It can't be very exciting. You run a long line through a hole, bait it, and then just leave it there. You don't even feel the fish bite."

I pointed out to my narrow-minded friend that despite such misconceptions, trotlining is one of the most exciting and time-honored methods of catfishing. No, you don't feel the fish strike. No, you don't experience the bend

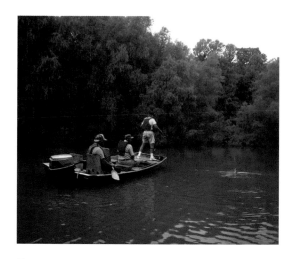

Some anglers can't imagine how trotlining could possibly be fun. But those who enjoy this time-honored method of catfishing say it can be just as exciting as catching a cat on rod and reel.

of the rod over a heavy fish. But trotlining offers its own special brand of excitement.

Adrenaline starts pumping as you paddle to your line. You shine your spotlight through the darkness, and when your marker is spotted, you make your way to one end of the set. Will the line hold any cats? How many will there be? Could this be the time when a monster will surface? The questions nag you as you lift the line and grab it.

You feel vibrations running through the trotline like an electric current. Yes, a cat has been caught—perhaps several cats. Your adrenaline rises even more as you pull your way past the empty hooks toward the one that holds your quarry.

Suddenly the water boils. The way it boils lets you know this is no little fish. To make such a disturbance, its tail must be the size of a Frisbee. You pull your way closer, and the catfish yanks hard against the line, almost ripping it from your hands. Your heart races. Beads of cold sweat run into your eyes.

Suddenly the water erupts, and you must brace yourself with a foot against the gunwale to keep from going in. You hold tight, keeping careful eye on the hooks dangling from the line and wondering all the while if it is possible to bring the monster in. The fish is thrashing the water, soaking you and your fishing partner and letting you know in no uncertain terms that it will not be taken without a fight.

Yes, my friends, trotlining is exciting. It is always exciting because it is shrouded in mystery and expectation. What's out there beneath the inky black surface of the water? What will you find when you lift the line? Sometimes it's nothing more than a few eating-sized cats. But that's OK. That's why you're there in the first place—to gather the makings for a fish fry. Still, you never know for sure what will surface next.

Giant blue cats, flatheads, and channel cats all fall for trotlining tactics. And as you might expect, heavyweight cats are much easier to subdue using the sturdy line and hooks of a trotline than with rod-and-reel outfits, which usually are unsuited for fishing lines heavier than fifty- to eighty-pound-test. Hook a sixty- to seventy-five-pound flathead in heavy cover and fast water, and it'll snap eighty-pound line like sewing thread. Hook it on a trotline made with 200-pound droplines and a 600-pound main line, and you might have a chance to land it.

Homemade Trotlines, Griffin Style

Ready-made trotlines can be purchased at many tackle distributors, or you can make your own like Ralph Griffin of Jonesboro, Arkansas. Like most dyed-in-the-wool trotliners, Ralph custom-makes all his lines, shunning inferior-quality, store-bought trotlines that come prepackaged and ready to fish. He shared with me his simple yet effective method for creating a sturdy and inexpensive trotline.

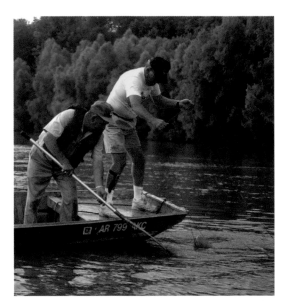

Ralph Griffin nets a dandy cat caught on a trotline in the Mississippi River. Although trotlines are frowned upon by some in the catfishing fraternity, their use dates back more than a century in this country, and where legal, they provide a fun means for catching numbers of nice cats.

"For the main line, I prefer #60 tarred nylon seine twine I purchase from Memphis Net & Twine," he said. "The coated line is more durable, and this size is heavy enough to hold big cats yet has the proper diameter for easy rigging."

This line is rated at 558-pound-test and costs about $5 per one-pound spool. "A one-pound spool is adequate to make one twenty- to twenty-five-hook line," Ralph continued. "All the lines I use have twenty-five hooks or less. The overall length of each line is determined by the size of the fishing area I want to cover with it."

To prevent catfish from twisting off, Ralph attaches 1/0 stainless-steel barrel swivels direct-ly to the main line. This is done by doubling a section of the main line between your fingers to form a loop six to eight inches long. Tie an overhand knot in the upper part of the loop to

Trotlines have numerous hooks, and several catfish may be caught each time the line is checked. Anglers should keep only the smaller fish they catch and only as many as they need to eat. It's important, as well, to follow special regulations regarding trotlines and to remove all lines after each use so they don't present a hazard to boaters and other anglers.

maintain the loop on the main line. Then run the end of the loop through the eye of a swivel and pass it over the end of the swivel. Cinch it tight with the swivel centered in the loop.

Droplines or "stagings"—short lines from which the hooks hang—are attached to the swivels. Ralph makes each one from a piece of #18 nylon line (170-pound-test) cut twelve to sixteen inches long.

"Each piece of line is doubled so the tag ends are together," Ralph instructs, "then you tie an overhand knot where the tag ends are and tighten it. Now, push a piece of this smaller line through the bottom eye of a swivel, pull it through, and loop it back through itself. When you draw it tight, you have a hanging loop of line six to eight inches long where you'll attach a hook."

Ralph prefers 5/0 stainless steel Limerick hooks. "This is just the right size for most of

As a safety precaution, the trotliner often wears a knife on his leg or keeps it in another easily accessible location. Should he somehow become hooked or entangled in the line, the knife might be a lifesaver.

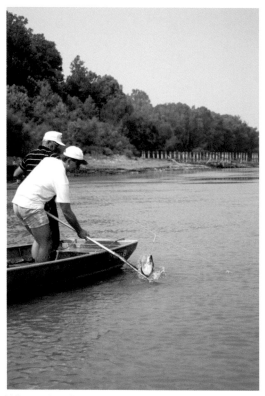

When checking a trotline, it's safer if you have another person to assist you. Dealing with multiple hooks on a weighted line can be dangerous if it's not done properly.

the fish we catch," he notes. "I use pliers to twist each hook slightly, so the barbed end is turned outward from the shank. I believe this increases the number of catfish I hook. The hooks must have large eyes that allow a doubled piece of #18 line to be pushed through them."

Each hook is attached by passing a dropline loop through the front of the hook's eye then looping it down around the hook point. The loop is cinched snug against the hook shank, and you're ready to rig another dropline and another and another until your line is the length you want it. The droplines should be spaced five to six feet apart along the main line.

Number and Placement of Lines
To increase the chance of success, Ralph often uses six or more lines all placed in areas he's scouted to identify as catfish hideouts. I have

accompanied him on many days to run his lines. His lines usually stretch from willows and other shoreline anchor points out into the river perpendicular to the current. The end of each is attached to a heavy weight to keep the current from swinging it into the bank. Because the trotlines are usually stretched from shallow water into deep, they cover a variety of water levels.

"With the lines set that way," Ralph says, "at least some of the hooks are going to be at the level catfish are feeding. If cats are feeding shallow, most of my catch will be on the shallow end of the lines. If more cats are feeding deep, the opposite will be true."

Ralph baits his lines with live fish. Goldfish or carp are preferred because they remain lively on the hook for extended periods, but shiners are used in a pinch and also produce well.

His tactics and trotlines work. Each year, Ralph catches many cats heavier than thirty pounds. His largest flathead to date was a fifty-seven-pounder and his biggest blue an eighty-four-pound monster.

"That one provided proof positive that the simple trotlines I make will hold the biggest cats," Ralph says proudly. "And they'll work for any catfishermen who puts them to the test."

Trotline Tips

When placing your line in a river or lake, take time to pinpoint prime areas, such as outside bends, tributary mouths, wooded flats, and creek channels where cats are likely to be lurking. Tie the line between two secure anchor points—from one snag to another, for example—then weight it in the middle or at a couple of points along its length to carry it near the bottom. Chunks of shad or skipjack herring probably make the best bait for large blue cats and channels. When fishing for flatheads, large frisky baitfish such as sunfish, goldfish, and carp outperform all else. Run your line every few hours to remove your catch and replenish lost bait.

Use special care when running your lines. Keep a sharp knife handy on your belt or strapped to your leg to cut the line if someone is accidentally hooked. Lines should always be removed when you leave so there's no chance another angler or animal might get tangled in the hooks.

Some say trotlining doesn't qualify as true angling at all. Others call it lazy man's fishing. A few go so far as to declare it unsporting. Nevertheless, trotlining is a traditional and legal method of catfishing in many areas. Done properly by conservation-minded anglers, it seldom hurts a catfish population.

Most of all, trotlining is fun. Before you condemn it, give it a try. You might get hooked.

Step-by-Step Instructions for Making a Trotline

1. Tie an overhand knot in the main line, leaving a six-inch dropper loop. Space the loops at five- to six-foot intervals along the line.

2. Attach a barrel swivel to the dropper by threading the dropper through the eye and back around the swivel.

3. Cut a twelve- to eighteen-inch piece of smaller diameter nylon line, double it, and tie an overhand knot with the tag ends.

4. Push the smaller line through the bottom eye of the swivel and loop it back through itself.

5. Add a hook by pushing the looped end of the smaller line through the hook eye then loop it back around the hook.

6. Finished droplines should be six to nine inches long and tied every five to six feet.

Snagging Cats

Only a hardened few are man enough to be snaggers.

In spring, they gather at the dams, standing shoulder to shoulder on the banks of muddy rivers. They come to fish, but to the uninitiated, their fishing seems foolhardy.

They use no bait. Their rods are extraordinarily long—sometimes more than sixteen feet—unwieldy, heavy. They cast huge weighted treble hooks far into the roiling water then snatch them through the water with hard jerks that jar their bones.

It looks like work. It is.

Cast. Reel. Snatch. Reel. Snatch. Reel. Snatch. Reel. Snatch.

Again. Cast. Reel. Snatch. Reel. Snatch. Reel. Snatch. Reel. Snatch.

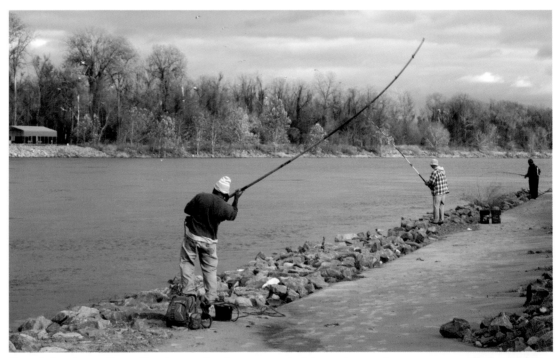

Dam tailwaters often attract crowds of snaggers in late spring and summer as catfish numbers swell when the fish migrate upstream.

They work the water with blind hope. They cannot see the fish they hope to catch. They do not know if the fish are even there. They know they will come though, huge numbers of them, as they have come for centuries, drawn upstream on their instinctual spawning migrations. Perhaps they are there already. Perhaps not. But come they will, sooner or later, in March or April or May or June, and when they stop at those concrete barricades, the snaggers will be there to greet them.

"How ya doing , Ol' Whiskerpuss? I cannot see you, but sometime today, or this week, or this month, after one snatch or ten thousand, my hook will bury in your flesh, and I will fight you and land you and take you home to eat. Until then, I will not be happy, I will not go away."

They are hardened men, these snaggers. You will not find among their ranks the fat, the flabby, or the out of shape. Their muscles are as hard and rippled as ironwood. I have never, in forty years among them, seen a woman in the mix. Nor a single yuppie. Farmers, yes. And carpenters and steel workers and factory laborers and river rats. Hardened individuals accustomed to back-breaking work. No wussies here.

The belly is their one weak spot if their tackle is an indicator, for covering the butt of each long rod is a split rubber ball used to soften the gouging their undersides must take. With each yank, the rod digs, the snagger winces. At day's end, they may be black and blue from breast to groin.

On a good day, if Lady Luck shines upon them, their rod doesn't break, their reel doesn't burn up, if a big cat doesn't spool them off, if the water is just so, the catfish are there, and if all else goes well, maybe, just maybe, they'll have a catfish or two to show for their labor.

Then again, maybe not.

The question taunts as you watch them. Why? Why do this? Why work so hard for so little gain? Why turn a relaxing sport into this form of masochism? Surely catfishing was never meant to be this way.

And so you walk up and ask one flat out, "Why do you do this?" And they reply—the same answer again and again:

"What's it to you?!"

Did I mention hardened? Hardened to the core. To the man.

I became a snagger for a while—had to try it for myself. Stood shoulder to shoulder with the tough guys lining the river banks below a local dam. Threw two eight-ounce snagging hooks with a sixteen-foot surf rod. Learned to cast seventy yards, sometimes more. And learned to stand there, hour after hour, day after day, casting, reeling, snatching, until I blackened my gut with bruises and could not turn the reel handle another revolution.

Once I snagged a catfish. It was, perhaps, the biggest I ever had on rod and reel. Spooled me off in thirty seconds flat. Zzzzzzzzzzz! Pow! That was it. Gone. 200 yards of fifty-pound mono. Never turned its head.

I wept. I quit.

Wussy, they said.

No doubt about it, snagging is a tough way to catch catfish. But in some states where the sport is legal, it appears to be growing in popularity. In my home state of Arkansas, below each of the twelve dams on the Arkansas River you will find on a nice spring day scores of snaggers flailing the water where just a few years before there were none. Why? I cannot say for sure. But if I were to make an educated guess, I would say it has something to do with the extraordinary challenge of it all. In today's world, people are looking for challenges. Skiing down Mount Everest. Jumping motorcycles across canyons. Sky diving. Bungee jumping. Competing in the Iron Man and Iditarod. Pushing the limits of human endurance and sanity.

Snaggers fit the mold. They see something that can't be done by average human standards, and they decide they must do it. And in the doing, they become addicted. Sweat and burning muscles fuel their fires. Doing things the easy way isn't in their nature. And that is why a shade-loving, bank-sitting wussy like me will never be a snagger.

And you? What about you? Think you want to try snagging? I've tried my best to talk you out of it, but no doubt, some of you will be inspired to give it a try. Guys like you never listen.

That being the case, here's the poop on snagging catfish.

Basics

In some parts of the country, the term snagging is seldom used. "Snatching" is a common moniker in many areas, and some folks prefer the term "blind-jerking." Whatever you call it,

A typical snagging rig: 10 ounces of lead and a giant treble hook.

however, wherever it is done, snagging works along the same basic lines.

Typical equipment consists of a ten- to sixteen-foot heavy-action saltwater rod, usually a surf rod, and a large-capacity bait-casting or spinning reel spooled with fifty- to 130-pound-test line. Two or three 8/0 to 14/0, needle-sharp treble hooks are tied tandem on the line, and a heavy weight up to twenty ounces is used to sink the hooks in swift tailwaters. Once on the bottom, the rig is jerked through the water until it hits a snag or a fish. Lots of terminal tackle is lost to logs and rocks, thus you will always see wise snaggers with an extra supply of hooks, sinkers, and line.

Snagging rods must be long so the snagger can better control his hooks and weights, which are frequently cast one hundred yards or more to provide greater coverage of the fishing area. Ideally, the snagging rig should move just inches above bottom when jerked by the fisherman—high enough to avoid entanglement with rocks and logs but not too high to miss catfish holding near the bottom. Long rods allow this type of retrieve.

Long rods also allow increased casting distance, which is important when bank fishing as most snaggers do. Snagging is possible from a boat, but unless the craft is extra wide and stable, the snagger's jerky movements can cause an upset. Long rods also provide extra hooksetting and fighting power, additional advantages important in this unusual sport.

Spinning reels seem to be preferred by most snaggers largely because of the increased casting distance they allow. But good bait-casting reels are tougher and provide more cranking power for big cats. The most important qualities regardless of the type you select are durability, large line capacity, and a good drag system. Select a model you're comfortable casting.

Fishing line takes a beating when snagging in cover-strewn waters, so abrasion resistance is an important characteristic. Most snaggers I've encountered use heavy monofilament. Quality brands are relatively inexpensive but offer superb blends of tensile strength, fairly low stretch, and high abrasion resistance. Dacron line also is popular and offers better hooksetting power.

Braided superlines also are gaining favor because their small diameter allows more to be spooled on a reel. Fifty-pound test has the diameter of twenty-five-pound mono, so you can pack more of it on, thus lessening your chance of getting spooled by a giant catfish. Although expensive, these lines have the lowest stretch of any line type, which makes them great for sticking hooks into trophy cats.

Treble hooks for snagging must be constructed of heavy durable wire and should be honed to needle-like sharpness before using and at regular intervals while fishing. Some snaggers use only one hook, but two or three is more typical. These may be tied to short droplines—attached to loop knots on the main line—above a terminal sinker. But most snaggers prefer to tie directly to the main line for more strength and most use specialty "snagging hooks," which are large trebles that have a conical lead weight molded around the shank. The weights on commercial snagging hooks come in a variety of sizes for use under varying conditions.

Done conventionally, snagging is back-breaking sport. There's a long cast to get the rig out in the river, a short delay for the weight to sink, then a violent backward jerk of the rod and quick reeling to recover slack line, another jerk and more rapid reeling, and so forth and so on until the line is reeled in. The angler then makes another cast followed by more jerking and reeling until, hopefully, a hook hits its mark.

Hundreds of casts may be made before a hook connects with a catfish, and there are times when the method is totally unproductive. I've also sat and watched snaggers catch catfish on every cast, including blues and flatheads up to eighty pounds. Timing is everything. When catfish numbers reach their peak in the water being fished, snagging is best.

When the efforts pay off and a catfish is on, there's plenty of exciting, white-knuckle action for the fortunate angler. If the catfish is hooked in the tail as often happens, the battle may be the most action-packed you've ever experienced. If it happens to be a big cat, as well, you're in for a rough and tumble ride.

I've seen many snaggers bury the hook in something solid, what seems like a log, and watched the astonishment on their faces when that log decided to swim away and take their gear with it. Mystery makes snagging fun—the mystery of wondering what will be hooked next. Sometimes it's a big paddlefish, an ancient river wanderer that may exceed one-hundred pounds. Because paddlefish feed exclusively on plankton, snagging is the only

Snagging can be back-breaking work. Long heavy rods are necessary for snatching the snagging rig through the water, and the angler may make hundreds of snatches for each fish caught. Good physical conditioning is a prerequisite for success.

reliable means for catching them. Often as not, however, it's a catfish the snagger snags, and even a ten-pounder puts up a whale of a fight when hooked this way.

Places & Times

Most snagging is done in dam tailwaters. There are two primary reasons for this.

First, astounding concentrations of catfish gather in tailwaters when their movements are impeded by dams. And in order to be even modestly effective, snaggers must ply waters where the densest congregations of fish occur. Snaggers fish tailwaters because cats gather there as thickly laid as fence pickets.

The second reason is a matter of legality. In most if not all of the few states where snagging is legal, this activity is restricted entirely to certain portions of various tailwaters. Lakes are off limits as are the main stems of rivers big and small. The snagger has no other choice of waters to fish.

The best season for snagging is spring or early summer. Catfish are drawn to tailwaters this time of year by an urge to procreate. As days grow longer and water warms, cats leave deep wintering holes and begin upstream runs toward spawning areas. Their runs are often stopped short by dams, and as the season progresses, the cats pile up. Some hardcore snaggers ply their favorite waters year-round, and modest numbers of cats may be taken any month. The height of the season, however, coincides with the peak of upstream runs. And if snagging is permitted by law during that time, that's when practitioners should be on the water.

Preparation

The best snaggers I've met have also been the best casters. I've seen some guys who could fire a snagging hook like a cannonball, casting it

Long casts increase the efficiency of the snagger, and powerful snatches make sure the hook buries in any fish that is struck. Note the tennis ball on the butt of this snagger's rod—added protection for his belly.

well past the mid-reaches of the Arkansas River, a distance of more than eighty yards. And always, they caught the most cats.

The reason long-distance casters are more effective is simple. They spend more time snagging and less time casting, working broad swaths of water on every cast.

With a little practice, you, too, can learn to cast great distances. The key is learning to "load" your rod. On your backswing, you must create a bow in the rod that will catapult your snagging rig when you bring your rod forward. You must also time your casting movements so your line is released at precisely the right moment on the forward swing. As in most things worth doing, practice makes perfect.

Recent Innovations

In Arkansas, many snaggers now use an unusual type of battery-powered reel to lessen

When these newfangled contraptions first started popping up in Arkansas a few years ago, they caused quite an uproar. People who saw snaggers with large batteries at their feet believed the snaggers might have created some new method of illegal electroshocking. Wildlife officers were barraged by phone calls from folks reporting these apparent law breakers. The devices are so commonplace now, however, that the furor has died down.

In talking with snaggers using the battery-operated reeling systems, I found no reliable source where the equipment could be purchased. Most snaggers, it seems, construct their own rigs in home shops or have friends who help them with tooling and construction. If snagging continues to increase in popularity, however, no doubt some enterprising individual will someday be mass-marketing these innovative rigs.

Conclusion

Before you try snagging, be sure to check local fishing regulations to determine if the practice is legal where you intend to fish. Snagging is illegal in many areas. And where it is legal, numerous restrictions are the rule. All catfishermen have an obligation to know and follow all regulations imposed on their sport. Without these restrictions, our catfishing resources would suffer.

If snagging is legal where you fish or if you're willing to travel somewhere that it is, then perhaps you might want to give it a try. Then again, maybe not. Like I said, this is not a sport for fat, flabby, or out of shape catters. If your idea of a fun outing is kicking back in the shade and taking a nap until a cat bites, snagging isn't likely to tickle your fancy. But if you enjoy a challenge, if sweat and burning muscle fuel your fire, then maybe snagging can provide a new way to liven your days on the water.

day's snaggers often use home-tooled cessories powered by batteries to reduce the involved in "blind-jerking" catfish. A push of the tton on the reel's handle brings in slack line, en the angler jerks again, hoping against hope to ry the hook in a fish he cannot see.

the amount of work required. Constructed from hand-machined parts and connected to a six-volt lawnmower battery, these reels have a button affixed to the rod handle that can be depressed with the angler's thumb. The snagging rig is cast, the angler takes up slack and makes his snatch, then the button is pushed to automatically reel up slack line before the next snatch. No turning of a reel handle is needed, thus the snagger's speed and efficiency are greatly improved.

Controversy

Snagging remains somewhat—often highly—controversial everywhere it is practiced. It is illegal in many states and restricted to certain seasons, certain waters, certain fish, and certain types of tackle in many others.

Arkansas, a state where snagging long has been practiced, offers a good example of the types of restrictions in effect in many states where snagging is allowed. Here, you may only snag gamefish, including catfish, when fishing from the bank within one hundred yards below a dam. You must keep any gamefish snagged and apply them to your daily limit, and you may not sell them. When snagging, you are limited to one half of the gamefish daily limit, although you may take a full limit of catfish and paddlefish, and once attained, you must cease snagging. Special restrictions apply to certain waters.

There is growing sentiment to stop snagging entirely in some areas where it is practiced. Many people believe it is an unsportsmanlike method for catching fish and that excessive numbers of fish are being harvested.

Studies conducted in areas where snagging is legal and popular do not support these contentions. For example, a survey conducted on two tailwaters on the Coosa River in Alabama found that "snagging catch rates were not excessive." Over a three-month period during the peak spring snagging season, the daily catch by snaggers averaged only about fifty fish. That worked out to less than one fish per hour per snagger. Only five to ten of those fish were catfish, and snaggers had to work several hours for each one caught. Snagging efforts and success dropped drastically during other seasons.

Is snagging unsportsmanlike? In the eyes of many, yes. In the eyes of others, definitely not.

If any practice can be shown to threaten our fish resources, then certainly we have an obligation to restrict that practice. But in areas where it has been studied, snagging catfish does not fit that criterion. It may be a bit different from the norm, but overall, snagging is simply another fun, exciting, legitimate method for harvesting catfish.

Noodling

To increase the excitement quotient on your next catfish trip, try catching 'em with your hands.

I know you will find it hard to believe that an intelligent guy such as me would even consider trying to catch a catfish barehanded while holding my breath underwater. It happened, though. Overwhelmed by a tsunami of beer-induced stupidity one day, I volunteered—yes, volunteered—to try my hand (literally) at noodling. I did so at the encouragement of my father-in-law, who was an ardent noodler for most of his eighty-one years, and my two brother-in-laws, who have been noodlers slightly less than half a century each.

"Folks may call you the dean of catfishing," they said, "but you're not the real dean until you catch a cat barehanded." Thus was I shamed into trying a pastime I had previously considered insane.

We noodled in a forty-acre private lake full of monster catfish, and specifically at a spot dubbed the "Hole-tel." When the lake was constructed in the 1930s, the owner, a man who is said to have loved noodling like some men love gambling or womanizing, created a vast field of concrete holes on the lake bottom in which his beloved whiskerfish could hide and spawn. This allowed him to walk out the front door of his home, wade into the water, and be noodling in less time than it takes to tell it. One of my brothers-in-law became the grandson-in-law

of this guy, and pretty soon all my noodling in-laws were visiting the Hole-tel on a regular basis.

And so, on this particular day, I waded out into neck-deep water, took a deep breath, and dove beneath the surface to a hole where my father-in-law had determined a catfish—so he said—was home. Then I reached in.

At this point when you first go noodling, many questions run through your mind. Why am I doing this? Will there be a snake in this hole or a snapping turtle? Do alligators live here? If a catfish is in the hole, will it bite me? How bad will it hurt?

They say big catfish will swallow your entire hand, start spinning, and shred the skin off your arm like a food processor shredding carrots. What will *that* feel like?

Extreme Sport

Catching catfish with your bare hands is an extreme sport by anyone's definition, ranking right up there with bull fighting, skiing Mount Everest, parachuting off waterfalls, and walking tightropes stretched between city skyscrapers. Several terms describe the practice. "Noodling" is almost universal, which is not surprising when you realize this is derived from the word

Author Keith Sutton wages war with a hand-caught blue cat. After his first noodling excursion, he swore he'd never do it again. But he did. Some dummies never learn.

"noodle," meaning a very stupid person—a fool. "Hogging" also is used, as are the synonyms "tickling," "grabbling," "grappling", and "graveling." In Nebraska, they call it "stumping," and in Kentucky, "dogging" is the preferred name.

It's hard to imagine the first brave person who reached underwater and probed a dark hole for dinner. But imagine it we must, for noodling leaves no traces. It is, as one writer describes it, "as ephemeral as some of the boasts it inspires."

Trader-historian James Adair was perhaps the first to leave a written record when, in 1775, he described "a surprising method of fishing under the edges of rocks" among Southern Indians.

"They pull off their red breeches, or their long slip of Stroud cloth, and wrapping it around their arm, so as to reach the lower part of the palm of their right hand, they dive under the rock where the cat-fish lie to shelter themselves from the scorching beams of the sun, and to watch for prey: as soon as those fierce aquatic animals see that tempting bait, they immediately seize it with the greatest violence, in order to swallow it. Then is the time for the diver to improve the favorable opportunity: he accordingly opens his hand, seizes the voracious fish by his tender parts, hath a sharp struggle with it … and at last brings it safe ashore."

Seized by the tender parts. I feared that might happen to me instead of the catfish. Nevertheless, I wasn't about to wuss out and look like a big sissy. Holding my breath, I felt blindly for the edge of the hole where the catfish lurked, slid my hand inside, and prayed my father-in-law wasn't pulling a prank on me that involved a snapping turtle or snake.

How to Noodle

Should you be "brave" enough to try noodling yourself, you will have to overcome the natural

Keith Sutton poses with the result of his hand-to-jaws combat. Noodling for catfish has become increasingly popular in recent years.

resistance normal people exhibit when told to stick their hand in a dark hole that might contain God knows what. You then must catch the fish inside.

The latter task often is much simpler than the first. When you reach inside the hidey-hole, the occupant, often a male catfish guarding its eggs, goes stark raving mad and bites your hands and fingers with a force similar to that you would feel if you accidentally bashed your fingers with a sledge hammer. All that is required of you is to find a way to surface with the creature in tow … without losing any digits or integument in the process.

The hole into which you reach may be an old muskrat or beaver burrow, a crevice beneath a rock, a hollow log, or any underwater cavity. Catfish occupy such holes at times year-round but especially during spawning season when laying, guarding, and fanning their eggs.

Most noodlers enter shallow water—never as deep as the noodler is tall—to probe likely catfish hideouts. Sometimes the hole is partially blocked with rocks, small sandbags, or the noodler's body to prevent the catfish's escape. If it is spawning season, however, this is unnecessary. Catfish guarding a nest seldom abandon it. When a hand is inserted, the fish may nip, bite, or if large enough, engulf the noodler's hand. The catfish may spin, causing the sandpaper-like teeth to shred the noodler's skin. For this reason, some noodlers wear gloves, although most believe this hinders the sense of touch necessary for determining the type of creature in the hole, its position, and the best method for grabbing it.

If a catfish attacks, the noodler attempts to grasp it by the mouth or gill cover. If it does not, as often happens outside spawning season, the noodler must make the catfish open its mouth so he can grab it. Wiggling one's fingers may do the trick, or "tickling" the fish

Noodlers catch cats bare-handed by reaching into spawning cavities where the male catfish guards its eggs. A big male may engulf the entire hand when it bites the offending appendage.

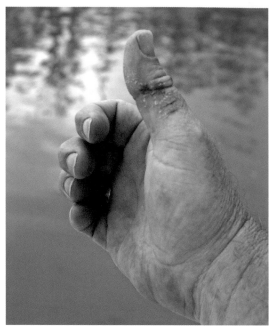

Noodling can be rough on the noodler's digits—the author's thumb after a blue cat chomped down on it.

Dangerous Sport

Check local regulations before noodling. In some states, it's illegal. In others, noodling is permitted but only with restrictions.

One also should consider the many inherent dangers. Crippling injuries can result. Reaching in holes can lead to serious cuts, so up-to-date tetanus shots are a must. If an arm or hand gets stuck or if an exceptionally large cat is tackled, the noodler can drown. Risks are high. Participants should be aware death or serious injury can result.

The closest most folks will come to hand-grabbing catfish is reaching across the table and grabbing a fried fillet off a plate. That's also dangerous but only when you're sharing a table with hungry friends and there's only one fillet left.

Me . . . well, I was stupid enough to try hand-grabbing the old-fashioned way. As I cautiously

under its chin. But sometimes the noodler must rely on feel to find the cat's mouth and forcefully insert his fingers. When a good grip is attained, the noodler attempts to resurface with the quarry.

At this point, the reason for working in shallow water becomes evident. If one cannot quickly stand with mouth and nostrils above the water, he might be in grave danger. Even then, battling a fifty-pound-plus catfish to the surface—and this is often done—may require extraordinary effort.

inserted my hand in that hole, I quickly dis-covered a catfish was home. It didn't bite. It didn't spin. Instead, it shot from the hole like a torpedo from a submarine tube and smashed into my chest. My friends on the shore above me saw big boils of bubbles rising to the sur-face as the air left my lungs. Then they watched, amazed, as a 250-pound man jumped from the water and onto the bank, much like a migrating salmon ascending a waterfall.

Blood dripped from my arm where the catfish's spines had brushed me.

"What happened?" my father-in-law asked.

"Something bit me," I said, breathlessly. "A snake or a snapping turtle, maybe. I'm finished noodling."

"Dean of catfishing, indeed," my brothers-in-law chortled.

I counted my fingers. Ten. I still had all ten.

My noodling adventure ended then and there.

Catfish Conservation

Why Catch and Release?

If you keep all the catfish you catch, it's time to change your ways.

"Catch-and-release catfishing": until recently, that term seemed to be an oxymoron, like "casual sex" and "non-alcoholic beer." Over the past couple of decades, however, more and more catfish anglers have joined the ranks of catch-and-release anglers. New regulations, such as slot limits and length limits, are responsible in some locales. But for the most part, I believe catfish fans, more conservation-minded than ever, have shown voluntary restraint. "Today's releases are tomorrow's trophies" has become the motto of many.

There are good reasons for this, reasons you should consider if you're still among the majority of catfish anglers who keep most of the fish you catch.

First, you're likely to enjoy better fishing for trophy-class catfish if you and your fellow anglers release larger specimens. Big catfish are

A channel cat like this 30-pounder may have grown for years before reaching its trophy potential. Releasing large catfish such as this helps protect stocks of heavyweight fish, thus enhancing trophy-fishing opportunities.

especially vulnerable to overharvest because when trophy-class cats are removed, it takes years to replace them.

Take flatheads for instance. Ten years are required to grow a thirty-pounder, even under the best circumstances. Flatheads exceeding fifty pounds are relatively rare individuals that may be twenty to thirty years old. If you remove a trophy flathead from a river or lake, decades may pass before it is replaced by a fish of comparable size.

Channel and blue catfish populations are similarly affected. Trophy fish are older uncommon fish. Yet many catfish anglers never consider releasing those they catch, especially big ones.

Small cats are much more common than big ones, so if you're fish hungry, keep some smaller ones to eat. There's no hard and fast rule to follow, but I personally draw the line at five pounds. The fillets and steaks I eat come from smaller catfish.

Resist the temptation to keep the heavyweights, and encourage others to do likewise. Shoot some photos, then carefully remove the hook and release the fish back into the water.

Release Right

When you do practice catch and release, be sure to do it right. Catfish are extremely hardy. An individual may live for hours out of the water. But if you expect a cat to survive following release, it's important to handle it properly. Follow these simple tips, and you can greatly increase the chances the fish you turn back will remain healthy and available for you or some other fisherman to catch again.

- Use circle hooks when catfishing. These tend to hook fish in the corner of the

When handling a catfish prior to its release, keep the fish in the water as much as possible while removing the hook.

mouth, vastly reducing mortality. Barbless circle hooks are even better. If you prefer other styles of hooks, use barbless models if possible or crimp the barbs with pliers.

- If a cat does swallow the hook, don't pull it out. Cut the line as close to the hook as possible, leaving the hook inside the fish.

- Bring the fish to the boat quickly—don't play the fish to total exhaustion while attempting to land it.

- Hold the fish in the water as much as possible when handling it, removing the hook, and preparing it for release. Want photos? Remove the fish briefly, and snap your shots quickly.

- Wet your hands so you don't remove the protective slime coating the fish.

- Use landing nets made with soft small mesh, such as salmon nets. These are easier on the catfish's smooth skin.

- Don't squeeze the fish or put your fingers in its gills. Cradle it in the water and move it back and forth to oxygenate the gills. When the fish is properly rested, it will swim from your hands.

The Red River Example

The best catfishing I ever enjoyed was on Manitoba's Red River, one of those rare catfish rivers where barbless hooks are required by law. The daily channel cat limit is four, none of which may exceed twenty-four inches. On a three-day fishing trip there, I caught around fifty channel cats, all of which were larger than any channel cat I had previously caught during a lifetime spent pursuing them. The smallest weighed approximately seventeen pounds, the largest approximately thirty-five pounds.

I have often wondered that if a river in Canada, where the growing season is short, can produce such tremendous numbers of trophy catfish, what might a similar river in the United States produce if similar fishing restrictions were placed upon it? If more catfish anglers practiced voluntary catch and release, if more of us push lawmakers to enact reasonable harvest restrictions, perhaps someday we'll have the answer to that question.

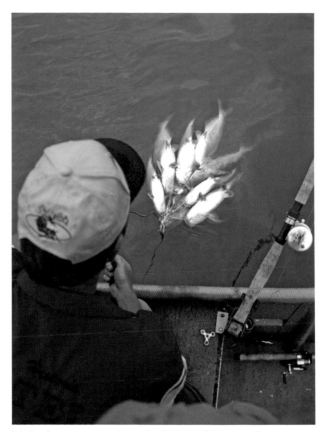

Today's conservation-minded anglers practice restrictive harvest, keeping smaller catfish to eat and releasing trophy specimens to be caught again.

Eating Catfish

Cats for the Pan

For most catfish anglers, eating the catch is the reason for fishing.

Catfish have been a staple of our cuisine throughout recorded history. Native Americans ate them, as did European explorers and the earliest settlers. In fact, our hankering for delicious catfish has done nothing but grow with catfish now among the most popular American food fishes.

While different types of catfish are very similar in flavor, catfish connoisseurs agree there are distinctive differences that make one species preferable over another for fastidious diners. In some cases, physical differences between species and size classes also necessitate differing

means of preparation to facilitate the utmost gustatory enjoyment of the catch.

These things being so, let's look individually at each species and its unique qualities. Knowing the differences will enable you to savor to the fullest these delectable freshwater fishes.

Channel Catfish

Let's begin our discussion with the most popular, most widespread, most abundant member of the family, the channel cat. Everywhere it swims, this species is targeted by a devoted group of anglers who like nothing better than

Cat anglers can be divided into two main groups: those who target trophy fish they will probably release and those who want to catch a mess of catfish they can keep and eat. The latter outnumber the former by a significant margin.

catching and eating this whiskered wonder. In states where catfish anglers have been surveyed, fifty to seventy-five percent prefer fishing for channel cats. And when asked to describe the number and size of catfish they preferred to catch and keep, most preferred four five-pound catfish or ten two-pound catfish over one twenty-pounder, a fact I think correlates to the belief that smaller catfish are more flavorful than heavyweights.

Most catfish anglers agree there's nothing tastier than just-caught catfish cooked and eaten by the water where they were caught.

When channel catfish are caught in extremely muddy, hot, or polluted waters, it is likely the flesh will have a poor taste. The same is true with other species of catfish. It is best, therefore, to concentrate fishing efforts where water quality is good and keep the catch alive or on ice until prepared for eating. I love the flaky white meat of all channel cats caught and cared for in this manner, but without doubt, the best tasting channel cats I've eaten were caught from icy cold lakes and ponds in winter and cooked fresh from the water over a campfire.

Blue Catfish

I once bet a friend fifty dollars he couldn't distinguish a fried blue cat fillet from a fried channel cat fillet in a blind taste test. My buddy was constantly saying a fat blue cat was better eating than any channel cat. But with a blindfold on and two plates full of channel cat fillets in front of him to sample (yes, just channel cats), he stated emphatically that plate number one must indeed be blue cat because of its distinctively better flavor. I graciously accepted payment of the wager.

Today's blue cat anglers handle big fish carefully to allow a healthy release. If fish are wanted for eating, smaller ones are kept.

Healthy populations of blue cats usually contain numerous individuals up to ten pounds. Larger older fish are much less common, but in some prime waters, catching several twenty- to forty-pound blues during a few hours is not considered unusual during peak fishing times. Specimens weighing fifty pounds or more are scarce and often difficult to find and catch, but more and more anglers enjoy the challenge of targeting these big hard-hitting trophies.

So what about those larger blue cats? Are they good to eat? I am often asked that question and always reply the same. Yes, they are delicious—a fact I confirmed many times in my younger, more ignorant days when I kept and ate every catfish I caught. Now I encourage fellow catfish anglers to practice restrictive harvest. Keep smaller fish to eat and release larger catfish—those that are older and less common—so they continue growing and providing trophy-fishing opportunities. There's no hard and fast rule to follow, but I personally draw the line at five pounds. The fillets and steaks I eat come from smaller, more abundant blue cats. Same with channel cats and flatheads.

Flatheads

When a mess of fish for the dinner table is wanted, the abundance of small flatheads in many waters makes it a cinch to load a cooler with plenty of eaters. And load the coolers we

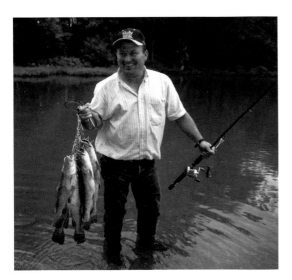

He's smiling because he knows these small flatheads are among the best eating fish in freshwater.

do, for many of us old cat men strongly believe a one- to five-pound flathead has a delectable flavor far superior to other catfish. I cannot say for sure why this should be, but flatheads scavenge much less than their brethren, preferring live foods, such as sunfish and crawdads, to the meals of dead fish or detritus blue and channel cats hastily devour. Perhaps it is this difference in diet that gives flatheads a taste many of us find much sweeter and flavorful. To me, it's like the difference between a fillet basted in butter during cooking and one that is not. The former titillates the taste buds in ways the latter cannot.

To heighten this savory flavor, one should always do two things when preparing a flathead—or any other catfish for that matter—for cooking. First, before skinning each fish, use a rope or nail to hang it head up from a support above a five-gallon bucket. Then use a knife to cut off the tail where it joins the body. Blood will pour out from a vein in the tail, thus "bleeding out" the fish, an endeavor that produces whiter, better tasting meat. The first time I tasted wild catfish bled in this fashion, I was amazed at the marked improvement in flavor.

Second, after you skin the fish, use a sharp knife to remove all dark red flesh along the fish's sides, particularly along the lateral line. This meat tends to have a strong, disagreeable flavor and contaminants that may be in the water where the catfish was caught tend to concentrate there. Get rid of it and the catfish not only tastes better, it's also healthier to eat.

Bullheads

Some anglers I know throw back all the bullheads they catch, claiming they have soft flesh and a disagreeable taste. Such is often the case when the fish are caught in muddy or polluted water or placed on a stringer to die in warm water. However, if you catch bullheads

Bullheads don't get very big, but a mess of small ones properly cleaned and prepared will provide several delicious meals.

in clean water and immediately place them on ice, they are delicious. Be sure to trim away all dark red meat on the sides, then roll the fillets in seasoned cornmeal and fry golden-brown for an entrée even jaded diners will enjoy.

Recipes for Catfish

For some folks, frying is the only way to cook a cat. There's simply no tastier method of preparation, so why bother with anything else? Case closed.

Truth is, versatility is one of catfish's greatest assets. Serve it fried, smoked, poached, baked, broiled, braised, sautéed, or barbecued. Or combine it with other foods for casseroles or chowders. Catfish can be eaten in a sandwich, a salad, a pizza, or an omelet. You're limited only by your imagination, as you'll see when perusing the many delicious recipes that follow.

The biggest mistake to avoid is overcooking. Catfish is naturally tender and cooks quickly. It's done when it flakes easily with a fork. If you wait for it to float in hot oil, you've probably cooked away the natural moisture that makes catfish so succulent and destroyed much of its unique flavor in the process. When deep-frying, heat the oil to 365 to 370 degrees Fahrenheit—no hotter. The old throw a match in the oil and wait till it lights trick rarely results in the proper frying temperature. Use a cooking thermometer to get it right or a deep-fryer that can be set at the correct heat.

Bon appétit!

Fried Catfish, Arkansas Style

This recipe can be used with any type of catfish and will feed a dozen or more people at your next home fish fry. The hot sauce/milk marinade adds a nice piquant flavor to the catfish without making it spicy hot.

6 pounds catfish steaks and/or fillets
3 (3-oz.) bottles Louisiana hot sauce
12 cups milk
3 cups yellow cornmeal
1 cup flour
2 tablespoons salt
1-1/2 teaspoons cayenne pepper
1-1/2 teaspoons garlic powder
Peanut oil

Marinate catfish one to two hours in a mixture of the hot sauce and milk. Remove fish and drain.

Combine the dry ingredients in a large plastic bag. Add the fish a little at a time and shake to coat.

Cook the fish in two inches of peanut oil in a deep fryer heated to 365 degrees Fahrenheit. Fry until the thickest part of the fish flakes easily with a fork, about five to six minutes. Remove and drain on paper towels. Repeat with remaining fish.

Serves twelve to fifteen.

Quick and Easy Grilled Catfish

This makes a delicious meal when you're in a hurry and cooking for two. Preparation is quick and simple, and the cooking time is just a few minutes. For more dinner guests, just multiply the amount of ingredients.

1 pound catfish fillets
3 tablespoons Worcestershire sauce
2 tablespoons lemon juice
1 clove garlic, crushed
1/2 teaspoon paprika
1/8 teaspoon ground black pepper
6 cherry tomatoes, halved lengthwise (optional)
2 green onions (optional)

Combine Worcestershire sauce, lemon juice, garlic, paprika, and pepper and pour over catfish fillets placed in a single layer in a large baking dish. Marinate in the refrigerator for two hours.

Transfer catfish to a large sheet of heavy-duty aluminum foil. Fold up the sides of the foil to form a rim. Pour the remaining marinade over the catfish. Garnish with tomato halves and green onions.

Grill over medium heat for about five to six minutes or until the catfish flakes easily when tested with a fork at the thickest part.

Serves two.

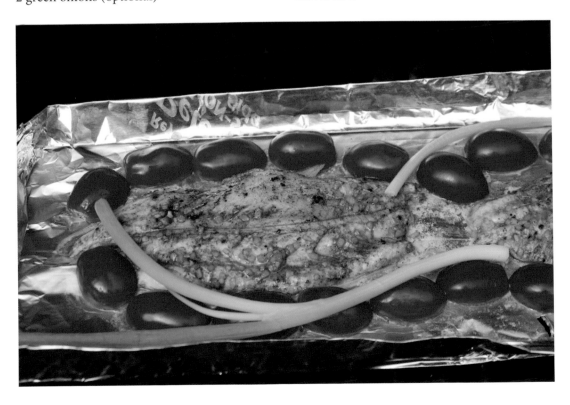

Blackened Catfish with Crawfish Sauce

This Cajun recipe is a real crowd pleaser. You can make it fiery hot by seasoning the fish heavily with the blackening spice and Tony Chachere's Seasoning or use less of these ingredients if you don't want your lips to burn when you eat. Either way, it's delicious!

4 (8-oz.) catfish fillets
Blackening spice (available in the supermarket spice section)
4 tablespoons butter or margarine
2 (10-3/4-oz.) cans condensed cream of shrimp soup
1 soup can half-and-half or milk
1 pound peeled, cooked crawfish tails
1 to 2 tablespoons Tony Chachere's Original Creole Seasoning
Chopped fresh parsley or cilantro for garnish

Season the catfish fillets to taste with the blackening spice. Heat the butter or margarine in a large nonstick skillet until bubbly, then add the catfish one piece at a time and sauté until crispy on the outside. Transfer to a warm plate. Add more butter to the skillet if necessary, and cook the remaining pieces of fish.

While the fish is cooking, prepare the sauce in a nonstick saucepan by combining the remaining ingredients except the garnish and heating over low heat until warmed through, stirring constantly. Do not allow to boil.

Serve the fish hot with a ladle full of sauce poured over each piece. Garnish if desired with chopped parsley or cilantro.

Serves four.

Lime-Broiled Catfish

Here's another delicious, time-saving recipe that makes the most of fresh catfish fillets. If you don't have limes available, lemons can be substituted.

2 pounds catfish fillets
1 cup melted butter or margarine
2 limes
Lemon pepper
Chopped fresh chives for garnish

Pour the hot melted butter in a large bowl, and dip each fish fillet. Transfer the fish to a rectangular pan lined with nonstick aluminum foil. Squeeze one half lime over each piece of fish, and season to taste with lemon pepper.

Place under a preheated broiler and cook six inches from the flame for three to four minutes or until the thickest part of each fillet flakes easily with a fork. Garnish with chives if desired, and serve immediately while the fish is still piping hot.

Serves four.

Cat Cakes with Dijon Sauce

When making these scrumptious fish cakes, adjust the ingredients if necessary to be sure they are moist enough to hold together but not so moist that they fall apart when cooked. And don't mess with the fish cakes when they're in the pan, or they'll break apart. Flip once during cooking. Cook a large batch if you like, then freeze some cakes by placing them on a sheet pan in your freezer for half an hour. Store them in freezer bags, and when you're ready to cook, take out as many as you need and defrost overnight in the refrigerator. They'll be ready to cook the next day.

1/2 cup vegetable oil
1 tablespoon chopped green pepper
4 tablespoons chopped green onion
1 pound catfish fillets, cooked, flaked
1 egg, beaten
1 tablespoon mayonnaise
6 tablespoons dry bread crumbs
1 teaspoon dry mustard

1/4 teaspoon ground black pepper
1/4 teaspoon cayenne pepper
1 teaspoon seasoned salt

Sauté green pepper and green onion in two tablespoons oil until soft. Drain. Mix with remaining ingredients. Chill for at least twenty minutes. Form into patties, and cook in the remaining oil until golden brown on each side. Serve with Dijon sauce.

Dijon Sauce
1/2 cup plain yogurt
3 tablespoons dry mustard
1/4 cup mayonnaise
1 tablespoon chopped green onion
2 tablespoons dill pickle relish
2 tablespoons balsamic vinegar

Mix all ingredients and chill until ready to serve. Serve at room temperature.

Serves four.

Catfish Gumbo

We often use catfish from the freezer to make this favorite on cold fall and winter days when we want something hot to warm our bellies.

½ cup chopped celery
½ cup chopped onion
½ cup chopped green pepper
1 clove garlic, minced
¼ cup vegetable oil
4 cups beef broth
1 (16-oz.) can peeled tomatoes
1 (10 oz.) package frozen sliced okra
2 teaspoons salt
1 teaspoon black pepper
¼ teaspoon thyme
1 bay leaf
Dash Louisiana hot sauce
1 pound catfish fillets
1-1/2 cups hot cooked rice

Cook celery, onion, green pepper, and garlic in oil until tender. Add broth, tomatoes, okra, and seasonings. Cover and simmer thirty minutes. Add catfish after cutting it into one-inch pieces. Cover and simmer fifteen minutes longer or until fish flakes easily. Remove bay leaf. Place a quarter-cup of rice in each of six soup bowls. Fill with gumbo.

Serves six.

Quick Baked Catfish

When time is of the essence, this easy recipe cooks up fast for a tasty dinner that's hard to beat.

2 pounds catfish fillets
½ cup mayonnaise
Bread crumbs
Paprika
Salt
Pepper

Lightly coat fillets with mayonnaise and roll in bread crumbs. Place in a baking dish coated with nonstick cooking spray, and season to taste with paprika, salt, and pepper. Bake in a preheated 450 degree Fahrenheit oven for about twelve minutes or until fish flakes easily when fork-tested.

Serves four to six.

Catfish Po'boys

We love sandwiches, and few are better than this Louisiana-style po'boy. For the best flavor, make it on fresh bread that's crusty on the outside and soft on the inside.

6 fried catfish fillets
6 French rolls
1 cup catsup
3 dashes Tabasco sauce
1 tablespoon prepared mustard
1 tablespoon minced onion
Dill pickles

Cut rolls in half lengthwise, scoop out the soft centers, and place in the oven until hot but not crispy. Combine ketchup, Tabasco, mustard, and onion. Spread the hot rolls with this mixture, then top with catfish, dill pickles, and the top of the roll.

Serves six.

Microwave Catfish, Potato, and Onion Casserole

For a delicious change of pace, whip up one of these quick and easy casseroles, a hearty one-dish meal that can be ready to eat in an hour or less. The cheesy taste makes it a family favorite.

4 medium potatoes
3 medium onions
1/2 cup melted butter
1 to 1-1/2 pounds catfish fillets
1 teaspoon salt
1 teaspoon black pepper
8 oz. sour cream
1 (10-3/4-oz) can cream of mushroom soup
1/2 cup dried bread crumbs
1/2 pound shredded Velveeta cheese
Paprika

Wrap potatoes and onions in plastic wrap and make a small vent hole in the wrap of each. Cook in a microwave oven for twelve minutes. Allow to cool and cut into slices. Lay the slices on all sides of a large square or rectangular baking dish and brush with butter.

Place fish fillets on the bottom of the dish, and season with salt and pepper. Mix the sour cream and mushroom soup and pour over all. Sprinkle on bread crumbs and Velveeta cheese, then season to taste with paprika. Microwave about eighteen minutes on high, then allow to sit about three minutes before serving.

Serves four.

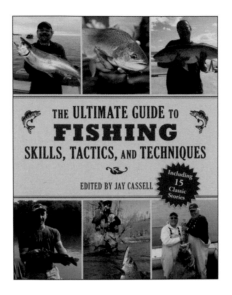

The Ultimate Guide to Fishing Skills, Tactics, and Techniques
A Comprehensive Guide to Catching Bass, Trout, Salmon, Walleyes, Panfish, Saltwater Gamefish, and Much More
Edited by Jay Cassell

With fishing advice from such experts as Bill Dance, Roland Martin, Wade Bourne, Tom Rosenbauer, Kirk Deeter, Charlie Meyer, Conway Bowman, and Lamar Underwood, *The Ultimate Guide to Fishing Skills, Tactics, and Techniques* profiles all of the major gamefish in both fresh and salt water and reveals pro secrets on how to catch them. Learn how Roland Martin entices largemouths with striking lures. Study Bill Dance's twenty tricks for consistently catching bass in thick weed beds or clear, open water. Want to know what Kirk Deeter and Charlie Meyer have learned from their years of fly fishing for trout? How about Lamar Underwood's tools for success? It's all here, divided into sections on bass, trout, walleyes, pike-pickerel-muskellunge, panfish, salmon, steelhead, catfish, ice fishing, and saltwater fishing for easy reference. You'll also find sections on knot tying, boats and boating, comfort and safety on the water, and even delicious recipes for cooking your fresh-caught fish.

This volume also includes a classic reading section featuring stories from such fishing literary legends as Nick Lyons, Ted Leeson, and John Taintor, who remind us what fishing is really all about.

$24.95 Paperback • ISBN 978-1-61608-561-2

ALSO AVAILABLE

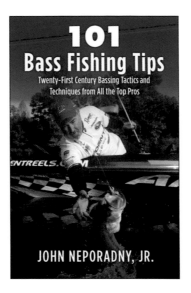

101 Bass Fishing Tips
Twenty-First Century Bassing Tactics and Techniques from All the Top Pros
by John Neporadny, Jr.

John Neporadny is an expert bass fisherman, and he's here to offer his secrets and those of other fishing greats on hooking hawg largemouths in *101 Bass Fishing Tips*. The latest techniques and tactics are revealed in this book full of tips from the top touring pros. The best competitors of the Bassmaster and FLW circuits share their secrets on how to catch largemouth bass throughout the year on various bodies of water.

Learn how to select the right tackle and lures so you can fish just like the pros. Bass fishing's elite anglers also discuss how to find fish on structures such as drop-offs, ledges, points, and flats. They also describe their tricks for coaxing bass out of weeds, bushes, stumps, docks, and other types of cover.

Beginners and advanced anglers alike will discover a treasure trove of valuable information they can apply on their favorite waters to catch America's most popular gamefish. Full of information and great stories, *101 Bass Fishing Tips* is the best guide available to help fishermen land more bass and is a revealing look at the exciting world of professional fishing.

$16.95 Paperback • ISBN 978-1-62087-792-0

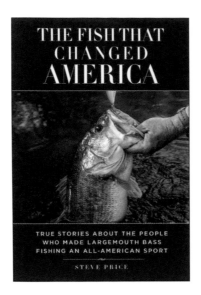

The Fish That Changed America
True Stories about the People Who Made Largemouth Bass Fishing an All-American Sport
by Steve Price

Bass fishing changed from pastime to business in part because of competitive tournaments and the publicity they generated. That publicity, in turn, sparked a demand for more and more information from the tournament fishermen themselves—how they caught bass—so in essence, the sport fed upon itself. Author Steve Price has interviewed dozens of anglers over the past few years, and he fits each of their stories into a complicated puzzle that forms a comprehensive tale of competitive record holders and fishing industry insiders alike.

The Fish That Changed America is not simply about tournament bass fishing, although some of the stories included here do involve competitive anglers. Rather, Price has tried to embrace a wider view of the entire sport and to show how different facets of bass fishing meshed so perfectly at the same time, leading to the state of the industry today. The participants—those who laid the foundation for what all bass anglers today enjoy—tell their own stories of what happened during those not-so-long-ago years. Many of the stories, such as the standing room–only funeral for a famous largemouth bass, touch on far-ranging topics that all anglers will enjoy.

$24.95 Hardcover • ISBN 978-1-62914-558-7

ALSO AVAILABLE

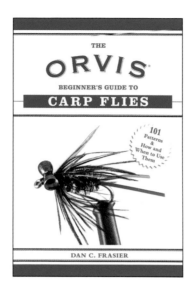

The Orvis Beginner's Guide to Carp Flies
101 Patterns & How and When to Use Them
by Dan C. Frasier

Carp are one of the most widely distributed and abundant fish in North America. Their prodigious size and habit of finning in shallow water make them appear to be easy fly-fishing targets. In reality, most anglers quickly discover that they are extremely difficult to hook on a fly. It takes years to discover how to catch them consistently. The reason? Carp can be very selective about what flies they will take.

This book will help to short-circuit that learning curve. Carp's selectivity can be boiled down to diet. Understanding what they are eating allows the angler to choose and tie a fly that will produce. *The Orvis Beginner's Guide to Carp Flies* walks the fly fisherman through the steps of identifying the most likely food source, illustrating the best patterns that imitate that food, and discussing how to effectively present those flies. With detailed information on tying all of the important carp flies, this book eliminates months of trial and error in your fly selection.

$12.95 Paperback • ISBN 978-1-62914-463-4

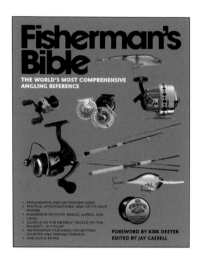

Fisherman's Bible

The World's Most Comprehensive Angling Reference

Edited by Jay Cassell

Foreword by Kirk Deeter

In the tradition of the bestselling *Shooter's Bible*, Skyhorse Publishing presents the *Fisherman's Bible*, the most complete reference guide for new fishing equipment and its specifications. Now, anglers will only need one book to discover all the new gear on the market as well as look up specs on accessories currently in production.

A comprehensive full color feature on new products includes large photographs of every rod, reel, and lure with extensive product details and feature listings. In addition to the latest gear, the *Fisherman's Bible* offers thousands of rods, reels, lures, and lines that have been in production and are currently on the market. All products are divided into fresh water and salt water, and further separated by spin, spincasting, baitcasting, and fly fishing. Nearly every fishing gear manufacturer in the world is included in this unique compendium.

With an introduction highlighting the hottest new products on the market, as well as timely features on such informative topics as new trends in fishing, a beginner's guide to fishing, and what and where to fish: popular species and prevailing methods, the *Fisherman's Bible* is an essential authority for any beginner or experienced angler, wherever he or she may live or choose to fish.

$29.95 Paperback • ISBN 978-1-61608-837-8

ALSO AVAILABLE

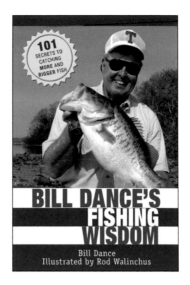

Bill Dance's Fishing Wisdom
101 Secrets to Catching More and Bigger Fish
by Bill Dance
Illustrated by Rod Walinchus

Bill Dance is one of America's best-known fishermen and has more than fifty years of on-water experience. *Bill Dance's Fishing Wisdom* combines his years of experience, knowledge, and wit into 101 tips that are sure to help any freshwater angler catch more and even bigger fish! Bill offers advice that might surprise even the most experienced fisherman, such as the importance of matching your line size to your lure when topwater fishing and how to prevent 75 percent of line failures with better knots. Complete with drawings by Rod Walinchus and color photographs, *Bill Dance's Fishing Wisdom* is key for any fisherman to have in his tackle box, boat, or lake cabin.

$16.95 Hardcover • ISBN 978-1-61608-267-3

ALSO AVAILABLE

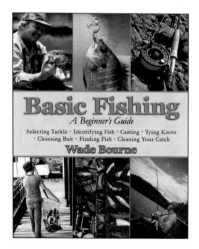

Basic Fishing
A Beginner's Guide
by Wade Bourne

New to fishing and have no idea how to start? With *Basic Fishing*, you'll be an accomplished angler in no time at all. Expert angler and award-winning outdoor writer Wade Bourne has created a step-by-step guide that masterfully breaks down the art of fishing with diagrams, vivid photographs, and lessons on:

- Different types of fishing equipment and how to select the best tackle
- Baiting techniques for artificial and natural baits
- Tips for selecting the best fishing spot
- Handy methods for cooking and cleaning fish

. . . and more!

$12.95 Hardcover • ISBN 978-1-61608-210-9

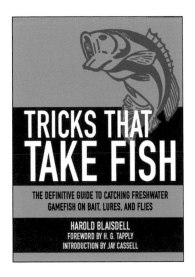

Tricks That Take Fish
The Definitive Guide to Catching Freshwater Gamefish on Bait, Lures, and Flies
by Harold Blaisdell
Foreword by H. G. Tapply
Introduction by Jay Cassell

Seasoned fisherman Harold Blaisdell shares the secrets he's discovered over years of catching trout, bass, salmon, pickerel, pike, and more. You name it, he's caught it. Here you'll find tips for catching trout with worms or minnows, attracting lake salmon with wet flies, making homemade decoys for ice fishing, and much more!

$9.95 Paperback • ISBN 978-1-61608-695-4